Our American Century

Dawn of the Century · 1900-1910

★

By the Editors of Time-Life Books, Alexandria, Virginia

Contents

★

22 The Cocksure Era

38 A Man's World
Masculine Pursuits

60 The Newcomers
The Changing Face of America

76 Flying Machines
An Ancient Dream Fulfilled

88 The Kids
The Joys and Perils of Childhood

104 The Old Hometown
Quiet Patience on the Prairie

118 Emerging Women
Home, Romance, Independence

140 Sports
Athletics Attract a Following

150 The Very Rich
An Era of Elegant Excess

172 Showtime
Entertainment for Everyone

188 *Acknowledgments*
Picture Credits

189 *Bibliography*

189 *Index*

Strollers enjoy the sand on Florida's Daytona Beach, about 1904.

A newsstand offers a wealth of information, New York City, after 1900.

Children help to deliver ice, Cleveland, around 1910.

Crowds enjoy the Fourth of July festivities, Nome, Alaska, 1901.

Minnesota farm workers take their lunch break, about 1900.

A horse disembarking from a barge on the Erie Canal requires special assistance, Durhamville, New York, about 1905.

A whirl of activity signals cotton-marketing day, Marietta, Georgia, 1905.

The finish of a transcontinental auto tour is cause for celebration, 1904.

The message emblazoned on New York's City Hall sums up the optimism of a forward-looking nation.

The Cocksure Era

It was a splendid time, a wonderful country. Most Americans felt that way as they welcomed the twentieth century, and many of them said so, with great animation and grandiose references to peace, prosperity, and progress.

From Senator Chauncey Depew of New York: "There is not a man here who does not feel 400 percent bigger in 1900 than he did in 1896, bigger intellectually, bigger hopefully, bigger patriotically."

Depew's colleague, Mark Hanna of Ohio: "Furnaces are glowing, spindles are singing their song. Happiness comes to us all with prosperity."

The Reverend Newell Dwight Hillis of Brooklyn: "Laws are becoming more just, rulers humane; music is becoming sweeter and books wiser."

"The will to grow was everywhere written large, and to grow at no matter what or whose expense."

Henry James

These statements set the mood for the first decade of the new century and won for the period several titles—the Age of Optimism, the Age of Confidence, the Age of Innocence. But another tag might have seemed more appropriate to an objective visitor from abroad: the Cocksure Era. For this was a time when Americans were optimistic and self-confident to an extreme; they did not merely hope for the best, they fully expected it. A welter of practical and moral problems—child labor, teeming slums, widespread offenses by corrupt politicians and ruthless corporations—could not shake the faith of Americans in the inevitability of their progress as individuals and as a nation. Most people automatically assumed that all problems would be solved in the normal course of events; meanwhile, the important thing was for a man to get ahead, to earn maximum returns from bountiful opportunities.

There was ample reason for high hopes and general satisfaction. The housewife found the stores well stocked and prices low; she could buy

A Native American chief gazes across the Bad Lands of South Dakota while his horse pauses for a drink. The photograph appeared in the first book of The North American Indians, Edward S. Curtis's 20-volume record of Indian life, which was published in 1907; sadly the way of life Curtis depicted was being destroyed by the country's rapid expansion and headlong economic growth.

America's "Great White Fleet" steams out of Hampton Roads, Virginia, in 1907 at the start of an around-the-globe journey, intended to impress upon the rest of the world the young nation's new status as a power to be reckoned with.

eggs for 12 cents a dozen, sirloin steak for 24 cents a pound, a turkey dinner for 20 cents. The farmer was doing well after some hard times in the 1890s. For the businessman, taxes were minimal and trade was brisk; indeed, conditions were almost good enough to justify the *Boston Herald*'s verdict, "If one could not have made money this past year, his case is hopeless." Everyone was fascinated by the many useful devices coming to the fore: the telephone, the typewriter and the sewing machine, the self-binding harvester and even the automobile (8,000 of these vehicles were registered by 1900). But to the thoughtful citizen, the surest portents of a brilliant future were the astonishing achievements of the recent American past.

In the nineteenth century, American energy and individualism had written a national epic without historic parallel. A thin fringe of eastern states with five million inhabitants had swelled into a continent-wide nation with a population of 76 million. In the 35 years since the Civil War, a predominantly agrarian country had vaulted from fourth place to first among the world's industrial powers; a loose collection of very different regions, administered by a laissez-faire government, had been woven into a fairly homogeneous and interdependent unit by expanding railroad networks, lengthening newspaper chains, and burgeoning techniques of mass production and nationwide marketing. And in just the past few years, the United States had fought and won an exhilarating war with Spain, emerging as a major military power with possessions and protectorates that sprawled from the Caribbean to the China Seas. The facts and figures—a veritable torrent of information on rich resources and soaring growth rates—promised that progress would continue at an accelerating speed.

Though no single fact could sum up America's past and present, the one that came closest was a casual item, appearing in the Census Bureau report for 1900, that brought brief fame to the small town of Columbus, Indiana. According to the report, the geographic center of population was now located near Columbus—a move of about 475 miles west since 1800. Implicit in the item were vast and ever-shifting patterns of

Officials walk among the rubble of the 1906 earthquake which shook San Francisco for 47 terrifying seconds, leveling more than 28,000 buildings and leaving half of the city's population homeless; the fires unleashed by the quake raged for three full days.

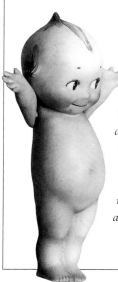

The wildly popular Kewpie doll, released in 1909, touched off one of America's earliest commercial crazes and launched a host of spinoffs, including Kewpie tableware and jewelry.

migration: the arrival and dispersal of 19 million immigrants; the conquest of the western frontier; the rise of big cities where forests and prairies once had stood ; the rise and decline of innumerable small towns—and, no less significant, the survival of countless towns and villages virtually unchanged in size and character, ideals, and biases. In progressing from the good old days to complex modern times, America was changing faster than its people knew, but it was also remaining much the same.

Clearly each community, whether rural or urban, was a special case, subject to a unique combination of forces. Old boom towns such as Creede, Colorado, petered out along with their payloads, while a corona of new towns in Minnesota attested to the discovery of the Mesabi iron-ore range. The commercial success of furniture factories in Grand Rapids, Michigan, cut into the business of country cabinetmakers as far east as Litchfield, Connecticut; the displaced rural artisans drifted into the cities to seek new work. But the most far-reaching influence on the pattern of settlement was the railroads.

For countless communities, the route of a railroad made the difference between growth and decay. Along the 193,368 miles of track that crisscrossed America in 1900, hundreds of hamlets survived or were jerry-built in the middle of nowhere, because they were needed to service the panting locomotives, which had to take on water every 40 miles or so. These forlorn way stations gave birth to some particularly graphic American slang: "tank town," "whistle stop," "jerkwater." On the other hand, many thriving inland ports, such as Little Falls on the Erie Canal and Paducah on the Ohio River, saw their dreams of greatness crushed, and were reduced to provincial towns, as manufacturers shifted their shipments from barge and steamboat to the faster rail freights. Even celebrated ports on the Mississippi were affected; Cairo and Hannibal and other towns suffered population losses traceable in large degree to the rise of St. Louis as a major railroad center. The decline of the Mississippi traffic was sudden and steep. The lifetime of one former river-pilot, Mark Twain, embraced both the heyday and the twilight of the palatial stern wheeler. "A strangely short life," said the author sadly, "for so magnificent a creature."

The statistics told an ominous story to rural America. While 60 percent of the U.S. population in 1900 lived on farms or in communities with less than 2,500 inhabitants, that percentage represented a nationwide shrinkage over the previous three decades. Rural New England had long since lost much of its population to the cities and to the Midwest; in turn, the rural Midwest had begun losing population to the cities and to the West as early as the 1870s. A survey of 6,291 small towns in five Midwestern states for the decade ending in 1890 revealed that 3,144 communities had recorded appreciable losses in population. By 1908, the continuing decline of the small town was causing such concern that President Theodore Roosevelt set up a commission to make an investigation.

Nevertheless, magazine articles announcing "The Doom of the Small Town" proved premature. It was true that many young men, attracted by the opportunities and excitement of the cities, departed on that classic journey by day coach to make a name or a fortune on the urban frontier; many rural towns, stripped of the most promising people, became, as an unfriendly observer put it, "fished-out ponds populated chiefly by bullheads and suckers." But at the same time many country towns attained a kind of stability and fulfilled useful purposes even in eclipse. Resolutely conservative in all things, they served as restraints on the pace of progress, as strongholds of the stern

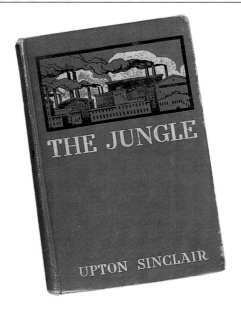

The Jungle, Upton Sinclair's exposé of the meat packing industry, was published in 1906, cutting meat sales by half and adding to the national fervor for reform of the nation's food and drug handling laws.

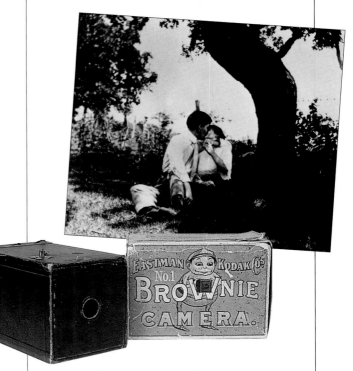

The Kodak Brownie camera (above) was introduced in 1900 at the modest price of one dollar, making it possible for ordinary Americans to take candid shots like the one above of young lovers sharing a tender moment.

old-time religion, as custodians of homely virtues and ideals taught to generations by McGuffey's *Readers,* as islands of security and leisure amid the hustle and hazards of modern times. In rural America God was surely in His heaven and all was right with the world.

Nostalgia for the country hometown staked a permanent claim on the American imagination. The close-knit relationships of rural life— that sense of belonging which author Zona Gale glorified under the name of "togetherness"—cast a spell on even those who had never lived in a small town. Five former country boys, yearning for lost togetherness in Chicago, manufactured an urban substitute in 1905; they founded the Rotary Club, whose membership grew in coldly impersonal cities from coast to coast. Many a man made a sentimental journey to his rural hometown, there to savor again its changeless peace and order, the kindness and informality of its people.

Despite the appeal of country towns, the cities grew ever more populous. They received a vastly disproportionate share of the 8.8 million immigrants who arrived in America during the decade. The newcomers, most of them poor Italians and Russians and Poles and Jews, found plenty of work in the mining towns of Pennsylvania and West Virginia, in the sweatshops of New York and Chicago, in the mills and plants of Pittsburgh, St. Louis, and Cincinnati. Here the newcomers also found plenty of countrymen; immigration in the nineteenth century had been so heavy that one third of the people in the United States in 1900 were foreign born or were the children of foreign born parents.

The cities bulged upward in skyscrapers and tall apartment houses, and outward in jumbles of slums and mansions, grimy factories and cheap-Jack entertainment centers. The population of three cities—New York, Chicago, and Philadelphia—had topped the million mark by 1900. Secondary cities—Cleveland, St. Louis, and Los Angeles—were much smaller but growing fast.

Growth rates could be used to form a general notion of the city's future, but they were inaccurate indicators. Nevertheless, at the turn of the century, when civic pride and boisterous optimism inspired a spate of futuristic articles and illustrations, local experts applied the figures with great self-confidence. Various New Yorkers, attempting to calculate

The nation's small-town past survived in places like Latham's Grocery in Dorrance, Kansas, population 281, in 1910. The prices for some of the staples (in bins, left), canned goods, and produce offered for sale are listed at far right.

Grocery Prices

Produce and Dairy Products
Red Apples   30¢ pk.
Dried Apricots   10¢ lb.
Seed Potatoes   35¢ bu.
Dried Prunes   5¢ lb.
Onion Sets   3 qt. 25¢
Eggs   12¢ doz.
Oranges   20¢ doz.
Butter   18¢ lb.
Lemons   15¢ doz.
Swiss Cheese   25¢ lb.

Housewares
Scrub Brush   15¢
Starch   10¢
Lye   5¢
Toilet Soap   3 for 15¢
Garden Seed   2 for 5¢
Candles   1 Box 15¢

Canned Goods
Golden Cream Corn 10¢
Boston Baked Beans   10¢
String Beans   10¢
Oysters   20¢
Tomatoes   20¢
Jams   10¢
Early June Peas   10¢
Green Turtle Meat $2.75
Sliced Peaches   25¢
Sardines in Oil   5¢

Staples
Tea 40¢
Sugar   100 lbs. $5.80
Coffee   15¢ lb.
Salt   100 lbs. 20¢
Cocoa   25¢
Salad Dressing   25¢
Macaroni   10¢
Baking Powder   10¢
Hominy Grits   10¢
Gelatine   15¢

A futuristic but prescient drawing done in 1900 portrays the New York City of 1999 crammed with skyscrapers, overflown by airships, and served by a network of bridges.

the population of their metropolis in the year 1999, arrived by way of the same statistics at predictions ranging anywhere from eight to 45 million. One oracle, noting that automobiles were shorter than horse-drawn vehicles and that auto engines were cleaner than horses, reached the wild conclusion that the cities of tomorrow would have immaculate streets and no traffic jams.

No one, not even the most imaginative prophet, could have predicted in 1900 what was about to happen to a sunbaked Oklahoma hamlet known locally as Tulsey town. Tulsey town itself might well have looked to the past rather than the future. Long an Indian meeting place, it was a small cowtown in 1900; its population was only 1,340, and the town consisted of a single dirt street lined with ramshackle buildings. According to the local press, freight-car business for the first week of

1900 was far from encouraging: "Receipts: one car bran; shipments: two cars hogs, one car sand, one car mules." The big story of the day was half business, half social event: Chief Frank Corndropper was soon to give his daughter Mary in marriage and to receive in return the groom's gift of several hundred ponies.

But 18 months later, Tulsey town—Tulsa—struck oil. By 1910, the population had soared to 18,182; 14 years later Tulsa would be a prosperous city of 110,000 inhabitants. Not everybody got rich, of course. But the career of one man was a fair index to Tulsa's success. James J. McGraw arrived as a poor boy in the land rush of 1893, and he rose with the town to become president of a bank, ensconced in offices in a 12-story skyscraper, doing an annual business of $40 million.

Even more spectacular was the growth of a planned city on the banks of the Calumet River in northern Indiana. In 1905, the site was 12.5 square miles of wasteland—rolling sand dunes covered with scrub oak. But late that year the city's namesake, Judge Elbert H. Gary, chairman of the board of United States Steel, poked a manicured finger at a map and told his directors, "This will be our metropolis. We'll build near the railroad junction of Chicago, where acres of land can be had almost for the asking, midway between the ore regions of the North and the coal regions of the South and East." The analysis was faultless and the city of Gary was christened before it was born.

The company's efforts soon proved once again that nothing could prevent American money and technology from working miracles. A bothersome river was moved a hundred yards. Great mechanical diggers chewed a mile-long harbor back from Lake Michigan; the major site was raised 15 feet with fill pumped in from the lake bottom. As railroad connections were forged, the jagged outlines of steel mills and foundries and tinplate plants rose against the sky. The final product was ready in July 1908. With proper ceremony, the first ore boat unloaded its cargo in Gary harbor and set the mills thundering. By 1910, Gary was an efficient corporative barony with a population of 16,802. That was Progress.

Or was it? A world of subtle difference separated true progress from mere change, and more and more Americans pondered the dimensions of that world as the decade wore on. Were urban phenomena like Gary and Tulsa and New York better places of habitation than the small town of Columbus, Indiana, or were they—as several grimly realistic novelists insisted—misbegotten work centers whose ugliness appalled the eye and whose labors crushed the human spirit with the mindless repetition of a

Unknown in the United States at the dawn of the century, Sigmund Freud (above) and Albert Einstein (below) would soon become as influential on this side of the Atlantic as they were in their native Europe. Einstein's special theory of relativity, published in 1907, revolutionized physics, while Freud's radical and often dark 1899 treatise on the nature of the human psyche, The Interpretation of Dreams, rocked and repelled much of the world.

single act on the production line? Did all their labor-saving, product-multiplying devices really improve the quality of American life? And was the work and wealth of modern industry divided equitably?

On this last count, the opponents of the status quo had a great deal to say. Muckraking journalists published angry exposés and backed their demands for reform with disturbing statistics. The average annual earnings of industrial workers in 1900 was a subsistence wage of less than $490; included in that figure were some 1.7 million children who labored for as little as 25 cents a day. One citizen out of eight lived in dire poverty in festering slums and perished of disease at about twice the rate of modest-income groups. In short, the reformers charged that labor was being exploited by an oligarchy of capitalists who lived in idle ostentation on annual incomes of many millions. The very rich said little in rebuttal, but one plutocrat did their cause no good by declaring arrogantly, "We own America; we got it, God knows how, but we intend to keep it."

Along these lines a battle was joined that would develop into a national crisis of social conscience. America's sense of justice and humanity, its treasured precept of equal opportunity for all, its jealously guarded tradition of free enterprise—all were called sharply into question. A free-swinging article in the *Atlanta Constitution* went so far as to say: "Government is no longer a vehicle for the enforcement of human rights but an agency for the furtherance of commercial interests."

Slowly, painfully, citizens faced up to the great civic work of twentieth century America: to make government more responsive to the needs and aspirations of the people; to reduce the discrepancies between lofty ideals and expedient practices, between good intentions and driving ambitions. That work had barely begun when the decade drew to a close. But it did begin. And that was Progress.

Yet if the sense of urgency was slow to grow, it was only natural to the time. For the great majority of people, the decade was a golden interlude, a long, comfortable moment before the good young days vanished completely and modern times arrived at full tide. Americans believed the judgments that confirmed their personal experience: that the human condition "is immensely improved and continually improving"; that "to stay in place in this country, you must keep moving"; that the average U.S. citizen possessed, and should enjoy, "the large cheerful average of health and success." It was generally true. Life for Americans from 1900 to 1910 was mellow and quite secure, full of vigor, savor, and fascination. All they had to do was go out and live it.

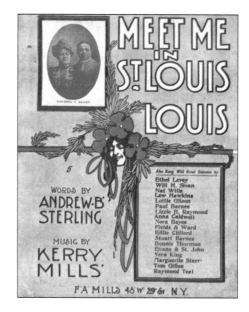

Americans' belief in unceasing progress was on spectacular display at the St. Louis World's Fair of 1904 (opposite), which attracted nearly 20 million visitors and inspired a hit song: "Meet Me in St. Louis Louis" (above).

"If you will meet me in St. Louis, Louis, meet me at the fair. Don't tell me the lights are shining any place but there. We will dance the hootchie-kootchie, you will be my tootsie-wootsie, if you will meet me in St. Louis, Louis, meet me at the fair."

From "Meet Me in St. Louis Louis"

Then and Now

When President McKinley proudly addressed the Congress at the turn of the century, America was a country very different from the colossus it was to become. The statistics of the period (imperfect though they were in those non-computerized times) illustrate the contrast dramatically. In 1900 there were only 45 states—despite the optimistic 48-star flag on page 13. The total U.S. population was 76,094,000. The average American worker earned 22¢ an hour. Automobiles were selling for about $1,550 each; and the truck and bus were still to be invented. In any case, fewer than 150 miles of paved highway existed in the whole United States.

Keeping up with the Joneses had not yet become a national religion. Only about 18 people in every 1,000 owned a telephone, and there was still no such thing as a radio, an electric icebox, a personal computer, or most of the other symbols of modern domestic consumership. People had other, more fundamental things to worry about. Diphtheria, typhoid, and malaria were among the leading causes of death. A cold might easily develop into pneumonia, and more often than not, pneumonia was fatal.

The most crowded occupation in the United States in 1900 was agriculture, for nearly 11 million people were farmers. But times were changing. Factory employment was already over six million and climbing fast; by 1996 it would top 18 million (page 36).

Nearly half a million immigrants poured into the country in 1900. These newcomers were bringing change with them, and by their ways and sheer numbers, too, they would help to cause change. By 1996, a year in which nearly a million more immigrants arrived on our shores, the effects of such change had become obvious and dramatic, as the figures in the chart on this and the following pages make clear.

Population	1900	1996
TOTAL UNITED STATES	76,094,000	248,710,000
URBAN (2500 or more)	30,160,000	187,053,000
Percent	40%	75%
RURAL	45,835,000	61,656,000
Percent	60%	25%
Native born white	56,595,000	*
Foreign born white	10,214,000	*
White	66,809,000	199,686,000
Black	8,834,000	29,986,000
American Indian	237,000	1,959,000
Asian	114,000	7,274,000
Hispanic	*	22,354,000

*Not available

STATES BY POPULATION

		1900	1996	Rank
1	New York	7,268,794	18,134,226	3
2	Pennsylvania	6,302,115	12,040,084	5
3	Illinois	4,821,550	11,845,316	6
4	Ohio	4,157,545	11,162,797	7
5	Missouri	3,106,665	5,363,669	16
6	Texas	3,048,710	19,091,207	2
7	Massachusetts	2,805,346	6,085,395	13
8	Indiana	2,516,462	5,828,090	14
9	Michigan	2,420,982	9,730,925	8
10	Iowa	2,231,853	2,848,033	30
11	Georgia	2,216,331	7,334,274	10
12	Kentucky	2,147,174	3,882,071	24
13	Wisconsin	2,069,042	5,146,199	18
14	Tennessee	2,020,616	5,307,381	17
15	North Carolina	1,893,810	7,309,055	11
16	New Jersey	1,883,669	8,001,850	9
17	Virginia	1,854,184	6,666,167	12
18	Alabama	1,828,697	4,287,178	23
19	Minnesota	1,751,394	4,648,596	20
20	Mississippi	1,551,270	2,710,750	31
21	California	1,485,053	31,857,646	1
22	Kansas	1,470,495	2,579,149	32
23	Louisiana	1,381,625	4,340,818	22
24	South Carolina	1,340,316	3,716,645	26
25	Arkansas	1,311,564	2,506,293	33
26	Maryland	1,188,044	5,060,296	19
27	Nebraska	1,066,300	1,648,696	37
28	West Virginia	958,800	1,820,407	35
29	Connecticut	908,420	3,267,293	28

STATES BY POPULATION (continued)

30	Maine	694,466	1,238,566	39
31	Colorado	539,700	3,816,179	25
32	Florida	528,542	14,418,917	4
33	Washington	518,103	5,519,525	15
34	Rhode Island	428,556	988,283	43
35	Oregon	413,536	3,196,313	29
36	New Hampshire	411,588	1,160,213	42
37	South Dakota	401,570	737,561	45
38	Oklahoma Territory*	398,331	3,295,315	27
39	Indian Territory*	392,060		
40	Vermont	343,641	586,461	49
41	North Dakota	319,146	642,633	47
42	Dist. of Columbia	278,718	539,279	–
43	Utah	276,749	2,017,573	34
44	Montana	243,329	876,684	44
45	New Mexico Territory**	195,310	1,711,256	36
46	Delaware	184,735	723,475	46
47	Idaho	161,772	1,187,597	40
48	Hawaii Territory**	154,001	1,182,948	41
49	Arizona Territory**	122,931	4,434,340	21
50	Wyoming	92,531	480,011	50
51	Alaska Territory**	63,592	604,966	48
52	Nevada	42,335	1,600,810	38

*Joined to become Oklahoma state 1907

**Became state after 1910

Immigration

	1900	1996
TOTAL ALL NATIONS	448,572	915,900
EUROPE		
Austria-Hungary	114,847	*
Italy	100,135	2,501
Russia and Baltic States	90,787	64,873
Ireland	35,730	1,731
Scandinavia	31,151	2,337
Germany	18,507	6,748
Great Britain	12,509	13,624
Romania	6,459	5,801
Portugal	4,234	2,984
Greece	3,771	1,183

*Includes part or all of Austria, Hungary,
the Czech Republic, Slovakia, Poland

Immigration (continued)

	1900	1996
ASIA		
Japan	12,635	6,011
Turkey	3,962	3,657
China	1,247	41,728
Vietnam	*	42,067
India	*	44,859
Philippines	*	55,876

*Negligible or not available

	1900	1996
AMERICAS		
West Indies and Miquelon	4,656	116,801*
Canada	396	15,825
Mexico	237	163,572
South America	124	61,769
Central America	42	44,289

*Includes all Caribbean nations

	1900	1996
AFRICA	30	52,889
AUSTRALIA AND NEW ZEALAND	214	2,750

Education

	1900	1996
ELEMENTARY AND SECONDARY SCHOOLS		
Enrollment	16,855,000	44,840,481
High school graduates	95,000	2,572,000
Total public school faculty	423,000	2,598,220
Average salary in public school	$325	$37,560
Cost per pupil	$17	$5,689
HIGHER EDUCATION		
Enrollment	238,000	15,226,000
Undergraduate	232,000	12,304,000
Graduate school	6,000	2,922,000
Faculty	23,868	869,000
ILLITERACY PERCENT	10.7%	less than .6%*

*New literacy measures instituted in 1981

Family Living

Family Living	1900	1996
Average size of family	4.7 persons	3.3 persons
Total families	16,188,000	69,594,000
Total divorces	56,000	1,150,000

Health

Health	1900	1996
AVERAGE LIFE EXPECTANCY	47.3 years	76.1 years
Male life expectancy	46.3 years	73.0 years
Female life expectancy	48.3 years	79.0 years
White life expectancy	47.6 years	76.8 years
Non-white life expectancy	33.0 years	*
Black life expectancy	*	70.3
All other races life expectancy	*	76.1
Birth rate per 1,000	32.3	14.8
Death rate per 1,000	17.2	4.9
Death rate per 1,000 under 1 year	162.4	7.7

*Data not available

CAUSES OF DEATH PER 100,000

	1900	1996
Heart-Artery-Kidney diseases	345.2	367.7
Influenza and pneumonia	202.2	31.3
Tuberculosis	194.4	0.5
Gastro-intestinal diseases	142.7	4.3
Cancer	64.0	203.4
Diphtheria	40.3	less than 0.1
Typhoid and paratyphoid	31.3	less than 0.1
Malaria	19.5	less than 0.1
Measles	13.3	less than 0.1
Whooping cough	12.2	less than 0.1
Suicide	10.2	11.9
Appendicitis	6.7	0.2
Childbirth	5.9	0.1
Total motor vehicle deaths	less than 100	43,900
Total executions	155	45
Total lynchings	115	none recorded

Labor

Labor	1900	1996
TOTAL WORKING FORCE	29,030,000	125,182,000
Men working	23,711,000	67,347,916
Women working	5,319,000	57,834,084
Percent unemployed	5%	5.4%

EMPLOYMENT BY MAJOR INDUSTRY

	1900	1996
Agriculture	10,710,000	3,400,000
Manufacturing	6,340,000	18,500,000
Service	3,210,000	34,400,000
Trade, finance, and real estate	2,760,000	35,200,000
Transportation and other utilities	2,100,000	6,300,000
Construction	1,660,000	5,400,000
Mining	760,000	600,000
Forestry and fisheries	210,000	25,981

SAMPLE OCCUPATIONS	1900	1996
Dressmakers (not factory)	413,000	97,000
Farmers	11,050,000	4,404,000*
Barbers and beauticians	133,000	822,000
Physicians	131,000	667,000
Bartenders	89,000	314,000
Domestic workers	1,740,000	1,201,000
Electricians	51,000	889,000
Telephone operators	19,000	164,000
Professional nurses	12,000	1,986,000

*Includes farm managers and operators

AVERAGE WAGE

	1900	1996
Per week	$12.74	$406.61
Per hour	$ 0.22	$ 11.82

	1900	1996
AVERAGE WORK WEEK (in hours)	59.0	34.7

Transportation	1900	1996
RAILROADS		
Passenger miles	16,038,000,000	8,371,288,000
Freight ton miles	141,597,000,000	1,421,000,000,000
No. of companies	1,224	68
Steam locomotives	37,463	none
Diesel/electric locomotives	200	23,500
Natural gas locomotives	none	2
SHIPS		
Total commercial ships	23,333	41,104
Steam tonnage	2,658,000	68,937,226
Sail tonnage	1,885,000	none
AUTOMOBILES		
Total registered cars	8,000	129,728,341
Total registered trucks and buses	none	76,636,815
Land speed record	65.79 mph	763 mph
Total miles of paved roads	under 150	3,912,226

TROLLEY CARS	1902	1996
Total miles of track	22,577	800
Vehicle miles	1,144,000,000	13,694,000

AVIATION		
Passenger miles	none	10.6 billion

Business	1900	1996
GROSS NATIONAL PRODUCT	$16.8 billion*	$7,580 billion
Goods	$8.42 billion	$2,177.3 billion
Services	$4.44 billion	$2,974.7 billion
Other	$3.89 billion	$5,152 billion
IMPORTS	$1.179 billion	$791.7 billion
EXPORTS	$1.686 billion	$624.7 billion

*Average over 5 year period 1897–1901

Communication	1900	1996
POST OFFICE		
Pieces of matter handled	7.13 billion	182.7 billion
PRINTING		
New books published	4,490	1,350,190*
Total daily newspapers	2,226	1,520
Circulation of daily newspapers	15,102,000	60,797,814

*From 9/97–9/98

TELEPHONE AND E-MAIL	1900	1996
Telephones per 1,000	17.6	769
E-Mail (daily)	none	34,000,000*

*America Online only

Government	1900	1996
GROSS DEBT	$1.263 billion	$5,355.0 billion
TOTAL RECEIPTS	$567,241,000	$1,453.1 billion
Internal revenue	$295,328,000	$1,408.9 billion
Customs revenue	$233,165,000	$18.7 billion
Miscellaneous	$38,748,000	$25.5 billion
TOTAL EXPENDITURES	$520,861,000	$1,560.3 billion
SURPLUS (DEFICIT)	$46,380,000	($107.3 billion)
TOTAL CIVILIAN EMPLOYEES	239,476*	16,866,000**
SALARIES		
Member of Congress	$5,000	$136,700
Cabinet member	$8,000	$148,400
Vice president	$8,000	$171,500
President	$50,000	$200,000

*1901 (1900 figure not available); **1995

A Man's World

★

MASCULINE PURSUITS

The men of the Trident Boat Club of Manchester, New Hampshire, meet for an impromptu band concert.

"The Master Sex"

I n any confrontation between the sexes, it was a foregone conclusion that men would come out ahead. For one thing, according to the 1900 census, men outnumbered women by more than a million and a half. But masculine supremacy went far beyond mere numbers. Like ex-President Grover Cleveland, every red-blooded American male was convinced that the sex he belonged to was innately superior.

The entire country, in fact, from the logging camps of Oregon to the U.S. Senate—with its convenient cuspidors—was seemingly arranged by men for their own satisfaction. Men ran the nation's business, cast its votes, and produced most of its art and literature. They were, in theory at least, complete masters of their households, dispensing justice and wisdom to their families like Asian potentates.

Along with their exalted status, men reserved special rights and privileges. Not only did they ban ladies from voting booths, they also kept them out of clubs, restaurants, saloons, and tobacco shops. In some states an unescorted female might, by law, be refused a meal at a restaurant or a room at a hotel, and in 1904 one particularly audacious young lady was arrested and put in jail in New York City for smoking a cigarette in public.

While men called the tune, they also worked hard to pay the piper. Most men labored at least 10 hours a day, six days a week. An office worker was usually at his stool by eight o'clock, a factory hand at his bench by seven. Both would remain there until five-thirty or six, when they would trudge home to pipe, slippers, and the affectionate ministrations of wife and children. All for an average weekly pay of less than $12.

In the confident mood of the first decade, however, most men were robustly certain that the opportunity to strike it rich lay just around the corner. With hard work and a bit of luck they might, like the Horatio Alger heroes, rise from clerk to president of the company. As good men, in an age of presumed male superiority, they deserved no less.

But whether he was a bank teller or a board chairman, the American male usually managed to fit himself out in a style that was suitable to a member of the privileged sex. He acquired clothing and accessories—such as the fancy shirts, silk hats, matchboxes and other articles shown at right and on the following pages—that solidly proclaimed his membership in the world of men.

"The relative positions to be assumed by man and woman in the working out of our civilization were assigned long ago by a higher intelligence than ours."

Grover Cleveland

Sartorial artifacts of the men's world of 1900 included detachable collar and cuffs, pocket watches, a silk hat, eyeglasses in a silver case, and a silver-headed cane.

The Dandy's Gear

The average man used an impressive array of grooming devices (above), to keep his hair sleek, his face smooth and his moustache trim. The most essential item was a folding, straight-edged razor with a wood or ivory handle (foreground, on top of mirror), which he honed on a leather strop (left, hanging from oak shaving cabinet). Using a brush of soft badger hair (on cup, foreground), he worked up a lather in a china shaving mug, which was often orna-mented with a personal insignia. The mugs in the cabinet include one bearing the owner's initials, another (middle of the center shelf) decorated with the emblem of the owner's fraternal organi-zation, the Elks. Aftershave lotion was kept in colorful glass bottles; cologne bottles were occasionally protected in boxwood cases (near blue aftershave bottles). For the hair and moustache, there was pomade (top shelf, at left)—and sometimes hair dye to preserve the youthful look that all men desired.

The Master's Toys

Most men's pleasures were fairly simple—a good cigar, a tot of whiskey, a poker game with friends—but the paraphernalia that went with them (above) was often elaborate. Cigar cutters took the shape of guillotines (rear center). There were oil lamps that both clipped and lighted a fragrant Havana (center, inscribed with an ad for Blaine Cigars). The majority of men chewed plug tobacco, and prided themselves on their talent for scoring a bull's-eye in a

shiny brass spittoon (right, holding cards). But cigars and pipes, from simple briars to elegantly carved meerschaums (foreground), were almost as popular. Whiskey was often kept in fancy crystal decanters that could be locked into a portable case (right, rear), or in handy breast-pocket flasks shaped like cigars (center foreground). Poker chips and counters for various other card and dice games ranged from conventional disks to rectangular counters and ivory fish (right foreground).

Manly Retreats

There is something mentally enervating in feminine companionship," advised *The Cosmopolitan* in 1905, and so "the genuine man feels that he must go off alone or with other men, out in the open air, as it were, roughing it among the rough, as a mental tonic." The spirit, if not the letter, of that statement was dogma at the time. Most men sought the society of other males in less rugged circumstances, in the comfortable, for-men-only atmosphere of barbershops, clubs, and saloons. A turn-of-the-century barbershop was much more than a place to get a haircut. It was a retreat where, amid the reek of cigar fumes and bay rum, men would congregate to browse through the spicy pages of the *Police Gazette,* ogle the ladies who hurried past the door, and wait for a 15-cent shave.

Even more secure from women were the men's clubs. For the rich and wellborn, there were such exclusive establishments as New York City's august Union League Club, whose major asset, according to one member, was the fact that "no women, no dogs, no Democrats, no reporters" could be found there. But most clubs were a good deal more proletarian. The average man could join sporting societies, volunteer fire companies, municipal bands and marching societies, and gourmandizing fraternities with such fancy names as the Honorable John McSorley Pickle, Beefsteak, Baseball Nine, and Chowder Club, which held raucous clambakes on an island in the East River in New York.

The most democratic gathering places of all were the saloons. There were at least 100,000 of these in the country, supplied by 3,000 breweries and distilleries. In Boston and Chicago, half the male population paid a daily visit to favored neighborhood bars. Part of the saloon's appeal was camaraderie, but the main attraction was the whiskey. So important was this commodity that on one occasion, when a supplier drew up to the door of a saloon with 20 large kegs of whiskey and a few small sacks of flour, one customer dryly commented, "Now what in hell does he think we're going to do with all that flour?"

Rudy Sohn's barber shop in Junction City, Kansas, with its reclining chairs and rows of shaving mugs on the wall, exuded an air of solid, masculine comfort.

The Cosmopolitan Saloon in Telluride, Colorado, featured roulette and a mahogany bar, which served whiskey as raw and rugged as the men who drank it.

Volunteer fire companies, like this one from Longmont, Colorado, often spent as much time training for races (above) with other towns as drilling for fires.

Crowned in laurel wreaths, an Olympian assemblage honors the theatrical promoter Harrison Grey Fiske (front row, third from left) at a lush dinner about 1901.

Men of Distinction

Much of the first decade's rhetoric about male superiority can be dismissed as simple sexism, a corollary to the demeaning attitude toward women then prevalent. Nonetheless, the decade did produce a number of men who left giant footprints on the terrain of history. Herewith a sampler of some of the era's most eminent men.

"It was a pleasure to deal with a man of high ideals, who scorned everything mean and base, and who also possessed those robust and hardy qualities of body and mind, for the lack of which no merely negative virtue can ever atone."

Theodore Roosevelt

Arctic explorer

Robert E. Peary drove a dogsled 400 miles from his ship in an attempt to become the first man on the North Pole. He completed his trek on April 6, 1909, in cold so intense that a flask of brandy carried under his parka froze solid. He marked the spot with the Stars and Stripes and the colors of the Red Cross, of the Navy League, of the Daughters of the American Revolution, and of Delta Kappa Epsilon (his college fraternity). Returning to civilization, Peary cabled his wife: "Have made good at last. I have the old Pole." Subsequent research has cast doubt on Peary's boast; some of his critics have even claimed that the spot he declared the North Pole was actually hundreds of miles to the south. Others continue to support his discovery of the Pole as valid. The controversy notwithstanding, Peary remains one of the century's most intrepid explorers. While accepting the National Geographic Society's first Hubbard Medal in 1906, Peary defined the explorer's mission (below).

The true explorer does his work not for any hope of rewards or honor, but because the thing he has set himself to do is a part of his very being, and must be accomplished for the sake of accomplishment, and he counts lightly hardships, risks, obstacles, if only they do not bar him from his goal.

Press czar

William Randolph Hearst ushered in the era of sensationalistic mass-circulation newspapers. After initial success with the San Francisco Examiner, he bought the failing New York Morning Journal in 1895 and made it the model of yellow journalism. Through the lavish use of photographs, splashy headlines, colored comics, a saber-rattling editorial policy, and some juicy scandals, he soon upped its circulation to an unprecedented 1.5 million copies—thus bringing more news to more Americans than any publisher before him. Never one to mince words, Randolph was less than charitable when describing the hopelessly out of touch doyens of journalism. When he acquired Cosmopolitan magazine in 1906, for example, he characterized the outgoing editors as "well-meaning and amazingly industrious persons writing without inspiration…able to pile before magazine readers indiscriminate masses of arid facts." For Hearst arid was unacceptable—only the sensational would do. It was a standard that journalism would embrace wholeheartedly in the years ahead.

Military man

General Leonard Wood was the stern symbol of a strong America during the country's colonial expansion. First a physician, then winner of a Congressional Medal of Honor in action against the Apaches in 1886, he later commanded U.S. troops during the Spanish-American War. Subsequently, as military governor of Cuba, he led the fight against yellow fever, built sewage systems, highways and railway lines, and devoted one-quarter of Cuba's revenues to the development of public schools. Among the many to revere him was his friend Theodore Roosevelt, who remembered General Wood when writing The Rough Riders (1899), excerpted below.

It was a pleasure to deal with a man of high ideals, who scorned everything mean and base, and who also possessed those robust and hardy qualities of body and mind, for the lack of which no merely negative virtue can ever atone. He was by nature a soldier of the highest type, and, like most natural soldiers, he was, of course, born with a keen longing for adventure; and, though an excellent doctor, what he really desired was the chance to lead men in some kind of hazard.

Beau ideal

Richard Harding Davis personified masculinity and derring-do. Novelist, journalist, man-about-town, he was known as the top war correspondent of his era. However, his flair for dramatic reporting was more than matched by his dashing appearance—square-jawed, clean shaven, stylish even on the battlefield. His personality was a strange mixture of vanity and self-mockery. "What I like most in men," he said, is the ability "to sit opposite a mirror at dinner and not look in it"—an ability he himself did not possess. In a letter to his mother (below), Davis revealed his emotional response to the suffering he witnessed as a correspondent during the Boer War.

Winston Churchill and I stood in front of Gen. White and cried for an hour. For the time you forgot Boers and the cause, or the lack of cause of it all, and saw only the side of it that was before you, the starving garrison relieved by men who had lost almost one out of every three in trying to help them. I was rather too previous in getting in and like everyone else who came from outside gave away everything I had so that now I'm as badly off as the rest of them.

Opposition champion

William Jennings Bryan led the underdog Democratic Party for almost two decades with a combination of shrewd cloakroom deals and compelling oratory. He ran three times for President but was beaten by Republicans McKinley and Taft. Even in defeat he was a tireless fighter for such lost causes as silver-based currency. He capped his famous Cross of Gold Speech (below) by attacking the gold standard with broadsides of Biblical locution:

It is the issue of 1776 over again. Our ancestors, when but three millions in number, had the courage to declare their political independence of every other nation; shall we, their descendants, when we have grown to seventy millions, declare that we are less independent than our forefathers? No, my friends, that will never be the verdict of our people. Therefore, we care not upon what lines the battle is fought. If they say bimetallism is good, but that we cannot have it until other nations help us, we reply that, instead of having a gold standard because England has, we will restore bimetallism, and then let England have bimetallism because the United States has it.... We will answer their demand for a gold standard by saying to them: You shall not press down upon the brow of labor this crown of thorns; you shall not crucify mankind upon a cross of gold.

Kingpin banker

J. Pierpont Morgan was the most powerful financier in American history. The very "embodiment of power and purpose," according to a fellow businessman, he used his uncanny business sense and formidable presence to create the world's largest corporation, U.S. Steel. Later, he singlehandedly saved the country from financial collapse in the panic of 1907 by holding 125 leading New York financiers under lock and key in his palatial library near Madison Avenue until they produced the capital to stave off disaster. Morgan's unfailing belief in his ability to get what he wanted was made clear in a conversation he had with fellow tycoon Andrew Carnegie years after Morgan's purchase of Carnegie's steel empire for a mere $420 million.

"I should have asked you another hundred million for those Carnegie properties," said Carnegie.

"If you had, I should have paid it," Morgan replied.

Leading educator

Booker T. Washington rose from slavery to found America's first college for black teachers, Tuskegee Institute in Alabama. Though resentment against black advancement ran high, President Theodore Roosevelt described Washington as the South's most distinguished citizen. When the president asked him to dinner at the White House, most Southerners were scandalized. In the face of such bigotry, Washington evinced no bitterness. "I shall never permit myself to stoop so low as to hate any man," he said. In the closing pages of his autogiography Up From Slavery he called for the world's compassion not only for former slaves, but for Southern whites as well.

The great human law that in the end recognizes and rewards merit is everlasting and universal. The outside world does not know, neither can it appreciate, the struggle that is constantly going on in the hearts of both the Southern white people and their former slaves to free themselves from racial prejudice; and while both races are thus struggling they should have the sympathy, the support, and the forbearance of the rest of the world.

The American Colossus

Among the notable men of his time, Theodore Roosevelt—soldier, statesman, author, adventurer, and advocate of the strenuous life—stood out above all others and left an unmistakable stamp on America. It was not physical stature, certainly, that made Roosevelt such a dominant figure. Dumpy-looking, his eyes heavily spectacled, a toothy smile protruding from under a walrus moustache, he cut an almost comical figure, somewhat like a cartoonist's rendition of an early Colonel Blimp. Neither was he a giant merely by birth—he was the son of a patrician Dutch family from New York City; nor because of his political office, the presidency. It was rather the dynamic force of his presence, together with his awesome energy, that made the magnetic Teddy stand larger in people's minds than any other man of his time. "His personality so crowds the room," said a friend, "that the walls are worn thin and threaten to burst outward."

Ebullient Personality: Everything about TR seemed bigger than life. He drank his coffee, with seven lumps of sugar, from a cup that, according to his eldest son, Teddy Jr., was "more in the nature of a bathtub." When he spoke, with a high-pitched, staccato bark, he became a "human volcano, roaring as only a human volcano can roar!—leading the laughter and singing and shouting, like a boy out of school, pounding the table with both noisy fists." He walked with such a fierce, determined stride that most people had to break into a dogtrot to keep up with him. "I always believe in going hard at everything," he wrote to his son Kermit. Nothing dampened his enthusiasm for rough-and-tumble. During a fox hunt in 1885, he fell off his horse and broke his arm. He remounted, finished the hunt, went out to dinner in the evening, and the next day tramped through the woods for three hours. "I like to drink the wine of life with brandy in it," he said.

This same unflagging vitality drove Roosevelt to the front line of public life. At age 24 he leaped into politics as a crusading Republican state assemblyman from New York City, determined to clean up political abuses in both parties. As New York City's police commissioner, he packed a pistol and patrolled the city streets to make sure his policemen kept busy catching criminals. With the outbreak of the Spanish-American War in 1898, he resigned his job as assistant secretary of the navy to lead a volunteer cavalry regiment, the Rough Riders, in a daredevil charge up San Juan Hill in Cuba. "I don't want to be in office during war," he said. "I want to be at the front."

Teddy's swashbuckling approach to public life often infuriated old-line politicians. The Republican national chairman, Mark Hanna, called him "that damned cowboy," and on the eve of TR's election as vice president under William McKinley in 1900, Hanna exclaimed in dismay, "Don't any of you realize there's only one life between that madman and the presidency?"

Accomplished President: Only six months after McKinley's inauguration, Hanna's fears were realized. In September 1901, an assassin's bullet took McKinley's life, and Teddy rattled by wagon down the trail from a mountain lodge in the Adirondacks to become, at age 42, the youngest President in American history.

President Theodore Roosevelt was the living embodiment of the optimism and energy of the country's mood. During his seven and a half years of vigorous, personal leadership, from 1901 to 1909, he wielded the powers of the Presidency as no man had done before. Roosevelt called his crusade the Square Deal, and the people loved it. They loved him for himself, too. "I have never known another person so vital," wrote author and editor William Allen White, speaking for the nation, "nor another man so dear."

Roosevelt plunged into the adventure of being president with the enthusiasm of a small boy embarking on a hayride. "You must always remember," said a British diplomat, "that the president is about six." But Teddy's accomplishments were man-sized. He acted to curb the power of the nation's huge trade monopolies and financial trusts—"malefactors of great wealth," as he called them. He arbitrated labor disputes, reformed railroad rates, pushed through a pure food and drug law and plucked 148 million acres of forest land from under the noses of lumbermen to create national parks. Wielding his famous "big stick" in foreign affairs, he battered down stubborn diplomatic obstacles to build the Panama Canal.

Inevitably, Roosevelt's energetic policies made him enemies. But though TR claimed he did not "care a rap for 'popularity' as such," the American people refused to believe him. His public appearances drew enthusiastic crowds. "Whenever he is in the neighborhood," wrote a commentator, "the public can no more look the other way than a small boy can turn his head from a circus parade followed by a steam calliope." Campaigning in 1904 on his platform of a Square Deal for every American, Teddy was re-elected for a second term by the largest plurality to date by a presidential candidate.

Doting Father: Despite his eagerness for action and adventure, Teddy Roosevelt, like most other males of the decade, was very much a family man. He had six children, whom he corraled for the solemn portrait below. But the normal mood of the first family was about as sedate as a public school recess. There were baseball games on the White House lawn, tag in the hallways and a menagerie of assorted pets that included dogs, rabbits,

Roosevelt sits for a 1903 portrait with his wife, Edith, and children (from left): Quentin, 5; Teddy Jr., 15; Archie, 9; Alice, 19; Kermit, 13; and Ethel, 11.

flying squirrels, a badger and a small black bear. According to one seasoned retainer, it was "the wildest scramble in the history of the White House."

Roosevelt, far from restraining the activities of his children, often took part himself. He engaged them in wrestling bouts, pillow fights, and football games. While at Sagamore Hill, the Roosevelt summer home near New York City, he took them on tramps through the woods and joined them in "romps" in the hayloft, although he admitted that it seemed "rather odd for a stout, elderly president to be bouncing over hay-ricks."

A Wide-ranging Mind: Roosevelt was more than an energetic demagogue in a cowboy hat. His intellectual interests seemed to touch the whole spectrum of human knowledge. "Whether the subject of the moment was political economy, the Greek drama, tropical fauna or flora, the Irish sagas, protective coloration in nature, metaphysics, the technique of football, or postfuturist painting," wrote the English statesman Viscount Lee, "he was equally at home with the experts." TR was himself such an authority on North American animal life that the professional zoologists at the Smithsonian Institution once called on him to identify a mystifying specimen of mammal in their collection.

Roosevelt's passion for reading was virtually insatiable. He consumed books at the rate of two or three a day, and he himself wrote 24 of them—histories, biographies, descriptions of cattle ranching and big game hunting, scholarly studies on natural history, and collections of speeches, magazine articles, and newspaper editorials. Sometimes his writing took on a rather moralistic tone; a friend once said, "If there is one thing more than any other for which I admire you, Theodore, it is your original discovery of the Ten Commandments." But the following excerpts, despite a certain pompous sense of right, reveal the determination, the vigor and the intelligence that made up the spirit of the decade's biggest man.

Roosevelt in His Own Words

Having been a sickly boy, with no natural bodily prowess, and having lived much at home, I was at first quite unable to hold my own when thrown into contact with other boys of rougher antecedents. I was nervous and timid. Yet from reading of the people I admired I felt a great admiration for men who were fearless and who could hold their own in the world, and I had a great desire to be like them.

I am only an average man but, by George, I work harder at it than the average man.

I have scant use for the type of sportsmanship which consists merely in looking on at the feats of someone else.

There are no words that can tell the hidden spirit of the wilderness, that can reveal its mystery, its melancholy, and its charm. There is delight in the hardy life of the open, in long rides rifle in hand, in the thrill of the fight with dangerous game. Apart from this, yet mingled with it, is the strong attraction of the silent places, of the large tropic moons, and the splendor of the new stars; where the wanderer sees the awful glory of sunrise and sunset in the wide waste spaces of the earth, unworn of man, and changed only by the slow change of the ages through time everlasting.

We demand that big business give the people a square deal; in return we must insist that when anyone engaged in big business honestly endeavors to do right he shall himself be given a square deal.

There is a homely adage which runs, "Speak softly and carry a big stick; you will go far."

Do not hit at all if it can be avoided, but never hit softly.

I wish to preach, not the doctrine of ignoble ease, but the doctrine of the strenuous life, the life of toil and effort, of labor and strife; to preach that highest form of success which comes, not to the man who desires mere easy peace, but to the man who does not shrink from danger, or from bitter toil, and who out of these wins the splendid ultimate triumph.

The White House is a bully pulpit.

For unflagging interest and enjoyment, a household of children, if things go reasonably well, certainly makes all other forms of success and achievement lose their importance by comparison.

Immigrants with baggage and identification tags land on Ellis Island, New York.

The Newcomers

★

THE CHANGING FACE OF AMERICA

The Immigrants' Ordeal

"Give me your tired, your poor, your huddled masses yearning to breathe free. Send . . . the homeless, tempest-tossed, to me, I lift my lamp beside the golden door!"

Inscription on the Statue of Liberty

Russian steamship ticket

Becoming an American," wrote a grateful but casehardened immigrant, "is a spiritual adventure of the most volcanic variety." Heedless of such cautionings, some nine million immigrants came knocking at America's "golden door" between 1900 and 1910. Many were so poor that they could barely scrape together their fare in steerage—sums as small as $12 for the voyage from Italy. But all were irresistibly drawn by the conviction that in America they would find what the old country had denied them.

What they found in America severely tested the immigrants' faith—and their courage and stamina as well. For most of the newcomers, the ordeal of Americanization began on a bleak scrap of real estate in New York harbor, Ellis Island. In 1907, more than a million immigrants poured through the island's overtaxed processing facilities. Once admitted to the "Land of Opportunity," most newcomers were doomed to years of toil (12-hour days and six- or seven-day weeks), at subsistence pay (an average of less than $12.50 a week), in the garment-making sweatshops of New York, in the coal mines of Wilkes-Barre, in the spinning mills of Fall River, and the grimy factories and slaughterhouses of Pittsburgh, Chicago, and other Midwestern cities.

Though the immigrants were welcomed by Americans of good will, they also met with plain and fancy prejudice. Xenophobic natives ridiculed their alien ways, and regarded them as subhuman animals. Men as influential as Senator Henry Cabot Lodge lent prestige to bigotry by insisting that the latter-day immigrants were inferior peoples whose prolific issue threatened the very foundations of Anglo-American civilization. No less a savant than Francis A. Walker, president of the Massachusetts Institute of Technology, was so seized by prejudice that he pronounced the newcomers "beaten men from beaten races; representing the worst failures in the struggle for existence. They have none of the ideas and aptitudes which belong to those who are descended from the tribes that met under the oak trees of old Germany to make laws and choose chieftains."

Disillusioned by bigotry and poverty, many immigrants gave up and returned home; 395,000 departed in 1908 alone. But the vast majority persevered. "Their hearts," said sociologist Charles B. Spahr, "cannot be alienated. The ideals, the opportunities of our democracy change the immigrants into a new order of men."

A mother and child, awaiting admission on Ellis Island, New York, are marked as immigrants by peasant garb—and the expression of hope, fear, and stoic patience.

An Immigrant Remembers

Among the hordes to arrive in America in that climactic year of immigration, 1907, was a small boy of 10 from Italy, Edward Corsi, who later became U.S. Commissioner of Immigration and Naturalization for New York. Corsi's tour of duty as an official on Ellis Island kept fresh the memory of his own childhood arrival there; years later he recalled *(below)* the October day that brought him and his family from shipboard in the hazy harbor to their new home in an East Side tenement.

"Mountains!" I cried to my brother. "Look at them!" "They're strange," he said. "Why don't they have snow on them?" He was craning his neck and standing on tiptoe to stare through the haze at the New York skyline.

A small boat, the General Putnam of the Immigration Service, carried us from the pier to Ellis Island. We took our places in the long line and went submissively through the routine of answering interpreters' questions and receiving medical examinations. We were in line early so we avoided the necessity of staying overnight, an ordeal which my mother had long been dreading. Soon we were permitted to pass through America's gateway.

Crossing the harbor on the ferry, I was first struck by the fact that American men did not wear beards. In contrast with my own countrymen I thought they looked almost like women. I felt we were superior to them. I saw my first negro.

Carrying our baggage, we walked across lower Manhattan and then climbed the steps leading to one of these marvellous trains. On this train I saw a Chinaman, queue and all! It had been a day of breathtaking surprises. I decided that anything might be true in this strange country.

Penned up by nationality, immigrants wait on Ellis Island. On an average day, 4,000 newcomers were processed, but 2,000 of them had to stay overnight.

Treasures From the Old World

Newly arrived at Ellis Island, a woman and her children clutch the few possessions that they carried with them on their voyage. Their luggage and bundles held treasures similar to those shown here—items considered too essential, or too dear to the heart, to be left behind.

Vest from Czechoslovakia

Crucifix from Russia

Socks from Italy

Shoes from China

Herbal remedy bottles
from China

Accordian
from Poland

Doll from Austria

Mandolin from Lithuania

Top from Portugal

The streets of New York's Lower East Side are filled to overflowing with the rapidly expanding immigrant population; an open-air market sells wares of every variety to the new arrivals.

Hard Lessons for Greenhorns

Bewildered at first by their strange new country, most immigrants stayed together in urban enclaves of their own. But once they had entered the Germantowns and Little Italys and Jewish ghettos, their fine new freedoms were often whittled away by the sharp edge of poverty.

Each ethnic slum was a tiny world that clutched at its denizens, holding them to a few filthy streets, markets and sweatshops. Seldom did the overworked laborer or his child-burdened wife have the will to venture a couple of miles to the wonderland of theaters and department stores. Elderly residents on the upper floors of tenements hesitated to attempt the ramshackle stairs; some did not leave their dingy flats for years.

The degradation of the slumdwellers triggered angry volleys from reform-minded muckrakers. Journalist Jacob Riis, himself an immigrant from Denmark, presented grim photographs and stories of festering tenements and their disease-ridden inmates; he warned his readers that "in the battle of the slum we win or we perish. There is no middle ground." Novelist Frank Norris, reporting on the Pennsylvania coal fields, described the lot of local immigrants: "They live in houses built of sheet-iron, and boards, about fifteen feet square and sunk about three feet in the ground. Of course there is but one room, and in this room the family—anywhere from six to ten humans—cooks, eats and sleeps."

Despite the long-term benefits of such exposés, the immigrants received almost no immediate improvement in their condition. Happily, there were exceptional cases, and a few city governments took steps to make life easier for the poor. Tom L. Johnson, the mayor of Cleveland, Ohio,

This Jacob Riis photograph captured the plight of transients crowded into a tenement on New York City's Bayard Street.

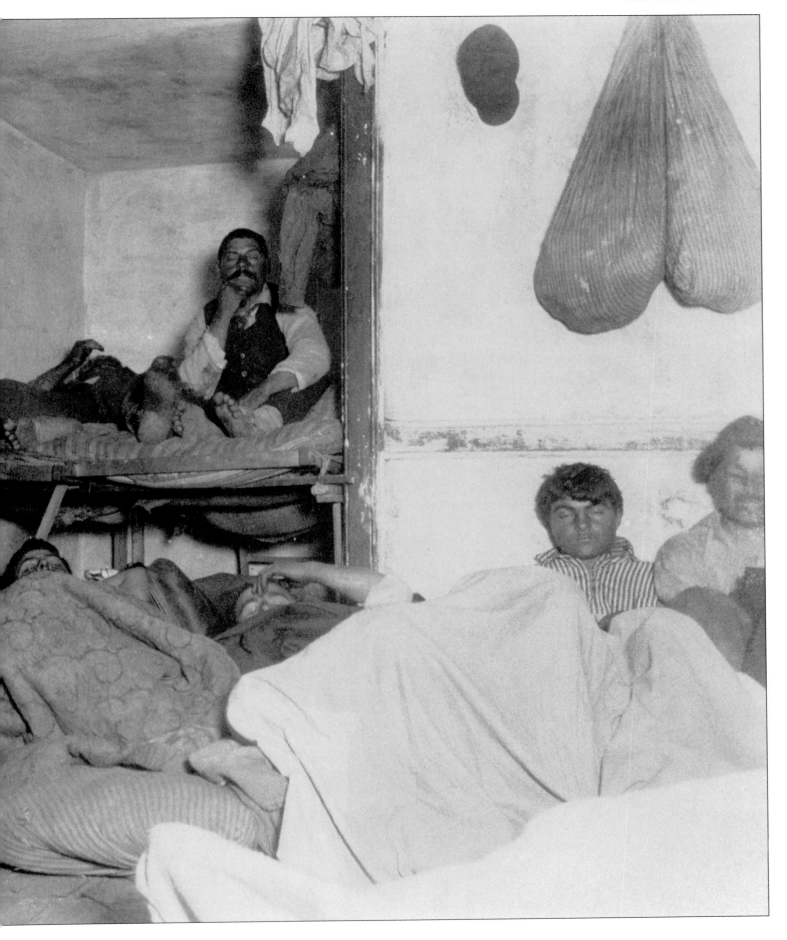

introduced cheap public transportation and built parks, playgrounds, and public baths to help brighten the dreariness of slum life. But in most other places, immigrants were forced to rely upon themselves. Banding together, they joined religious brotherhoods, community welfare associations, labor unions and local political clubs.

Politically, most of the newcomers were inexperienced and naive; they spent years learning how to use the American party system. In the interim, many became the clients—and the victims—of machine politicians, who, although they did offer some leadership and protection, nevertheless set records for venality and greed.

Because many of the big-city political bosses were immigrants with immigrant followings, bigoted natives held the newcomers responsible for political corruption. But the muckraking champions of the hapless immigrant put bossism in proper perspective. Lincoln Steffens, investigating municipal corruption for a series in *McClure's* magazine, found New York and Chicago well governed despite their immigrants, while Philadelphia, "the purest American community of all," was "the most hopeless." Steffens concluded: "The 'foreign element' excuse is one of the hypocritical lies that save us from the clear sight of ourselves."

The prejudice and scorn of natives drove many immigrants in upon themselves and hardened them. However, most of the younger immigrants, and almost all of the second generation, sought to win acceptance by Americanization. They were eager to abandon Old World ways and dress, to speak English without an accent, to acquire American friends and manners. Some parents encouraged their children's efforts to Americanize. Others resisted with the full strength of their Old World authority. But in either case, the results were usually the same. Even before the children grew up and left home, they drifted away from the family, and the gap between the generations steadily widened.

Countless immigrants escaped from the slums and into the American mainstream. But they left behind many others—people once as optimistic as they—to hopeless poverty and frustration.

Staring blankly, a young woman pauses in her kitchen amid evidence of her hard fate: a broken faucet, an abandoned boot, a littered floor.

Doing "home work" in the dreary confines of their New York tenement, an Italian immigrant family earns a precarious living by making artificial flowers.

Orville Wright makes the first airplane flight, while brother Wilbur trots alongside.

Flying Machines

AN ANCIENT DREAM FULFILLED

"Aerial flight is one of that class of problems with which man can never cope."

Simon Newcomb, 1903

Orville Wright

Wilbur Wright

A $50,000 disaster, Samuel Langley's airplane caught a wing tip on its catapult and broke apart in mid-air before plummeting into the Potomac River.

A Decade of Ups and Downs

In the year 1903, almost nobody believed that human beings would ever fly. Most people agreed with the noted astronomer, Simon Newcomb, when he said that it was just common sense to keep both feet firmly planted on the ground.

At least two men knew better. In December 1903, on a sandspit at Kitty Hawk, North Carolina, Orville and Wilbur Wright were putting the finishing touches on a "whopper flying machine" they had built at their bicycle shop in Dayton, Ohio, and shipped to Kitty Hawk for tests. Confident of success, Orville sent a telegram to his father in Dayton urging secrecy. Then quite suddenly on December 17 the deed was done. The two brothers piloted their flimsy, jerry-built machine on a series of wobbly flights, the longest one lasting 59 seconds and covering 852 feet.

The next day, only two newspapers in the entire United States saw fit to carry the story. Other papers were still grousing over an earlier flight attempt that seemed to confirm the national suspicion that the sky was a place only for birds, angels, and fools. Just nine days before Kitty Hawk, the secretary of the Smithsonian Institution, Samuel Langley, had tried to launch a winged contraption from the roof of a houseboat on the Potomac River in Washington, D.C. Langley, backed by a $50,000 grant from the War Department, had spent five years perfecting his machine. But while boatloads of reporters and government officials watched expectantly, the craft left its catapult and plunged nose first *(opposite)* into the Potomac.

Most people's interest in aviation took a nosedive along with Langley's pioneering machine. Not until 1908, after Wilbur and Orville demonstrated an improved version of their airplane to U.S. government officials, did the public awaken to the fact that men were truly flying. Then it seemed that everyone wanted to get into the air.

Across the country, inspired backyard aeronauts started building their own weird-looking contraptions, all designed to go the Wrights one better. Sportsmen and military daredevils mingled at fashionable air meets. As this whirl of airborne activity got under way, Wilbur Wright observed soberly that "the age of flight had come at last." Indeed it had, but there was still no agreement whatever *(following pages)* on the best way for man to stay aloft, now that he had finally gotten there.

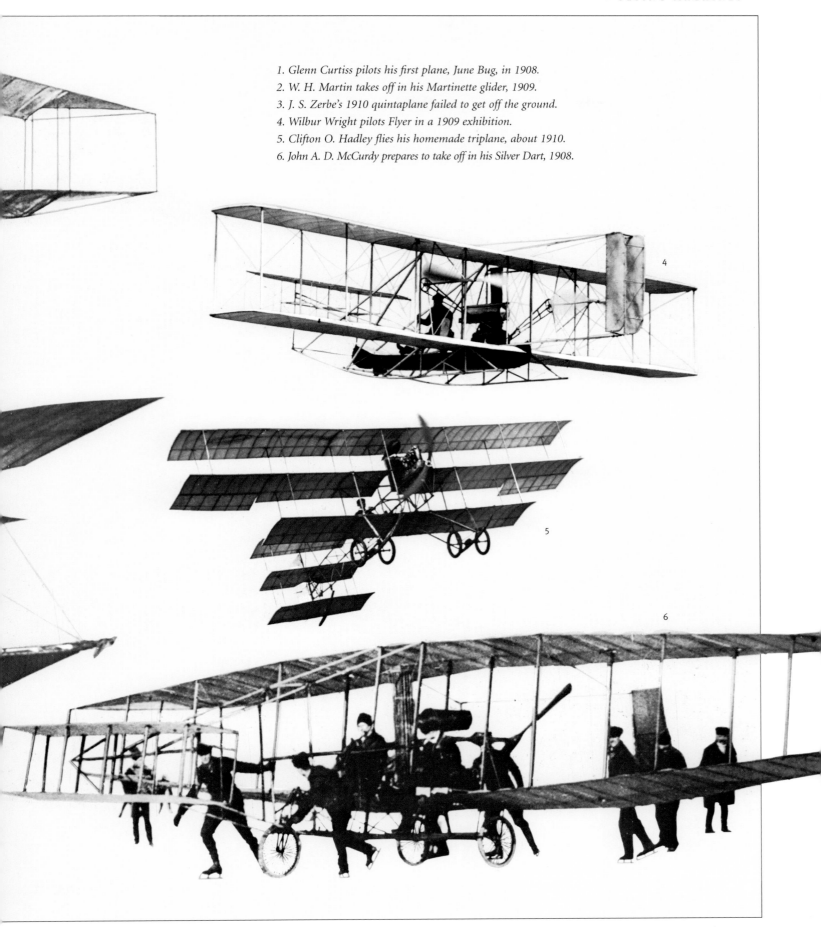

1. *Glenn Curtiss pilots his first plane, June Bug, in 1908.*
2. *W. H. Martin takes off in his Martinette glider, 1909.*
3. *J. S. Zerbe's 1910 quintaplane failed to get off the ground.*
4. *Wilbur Wright pilots Flyer in a 1909 exhibition.*
5. *Clifton O. Hadley flies his homemade triplane, about 1910.*
6. *John A. D. McCurdy prepares to take off in his Silver Dart, 1908.*

Despite its two imposing overhead rotors, this prototype helicopter hammered together by the blacksmith of Jetmore, Kansas, never made it off the town's main street.

A Grand Old Gasbag

While newborn planes were staggering aloft, an even more unlikely type of aircraft began to drift across the skies. It was called the dirigible, and it was a gas-filled, sausage-shaped balloon propelled by an engine. The most precocious dirigible builder of the decade was 14-year-old Cromwell Dixon *(left, top)* of Columbus, Ohio, who designed and actually flew several airships, including one model that could be driven through the sky like a bicycle, by pedaling. In the following letter to *St. Nicholas* magazine, Dixon's proud mother *(left, bottom)* describes the fortitude of the youthful aeronaut.

Dear St. Nicholas
Columbus, Ohio

As I attend to my son Cromwell's business, I will write you a few lines pertaining to his work, and also send you some very good photographs of Cromwell himself and his sky-bicycle and of his air-ship. Most people prefer the sky-bicycle, as it was the little fellow's own invention and he built it himself, even cutting the silk for the gas-bag over a pattern that Mr. Knabenshue, the great Toledo aeronaut, cut for him. I stitched it and we both worked night and day until it was finished. Then we varnished it. We had to be very careful for if we had not watched it carefully it would have stuck together so tightly that we could not have gotten it apart, but after several days it dried sufficiently to put on another coat, and so on until we had five coats. Then we kept it inflated until the last coat was dry. Cromwell was happy then, as he could get ready to test his sky-bicycle.

Then while at one of the Columbus parks, where Cromwell was engaged to make a flight, he lost everything he had by fire, so all had to be done over again. He went to work and made the second outfit even better than the first, so you see what a brave little man he was. Not even a sigh, when all he had accomplished lay a heap of ashes. He turned to me and said: "Well, mother, we must commence tomorrow on our new outfit so that we can fulfill our engagements this summer."

Cromwell has always been of a mechanical nature. Having shown his preference for such things, I encouraged him, and helped him besides. He lost his father when a baby.

He attended the St. Louis balloon and air-ship carnival, where Cromwell was a great favorite and where he made a beautiful flight in his sky-cycle.

Very truly yours,
Mrs. C. Dixon

The living image of a Halloween fantasy, Mrs. Cromwell Dixon guides a gasoline-powered dirigible pasted and screwed together by her 14-year-old son.

The U.S. Army's first aircraft was this dirigible, bought in 1908. But since no one could fly it except its inventor, T. S. Baldwin (near tail), it was never used.

The Kids

★

A glum crew of young students endures the flag drill in a school pageant.

The Grownups Close In

The first decade was a watershed in the special world of the young. In keeping with the Victorian era just past, the decade began as a time of strict rules and frequent moralizing. At home, fathers were not inclined to spare the rod, and at the dinner table children were well scrubbed and not heard. In the classroom, whispering was an offense that merited a whipping. Sunday-school teachers darkly noted that erring mortals had once been punished with Noah's flood, and that next time God planned to finish the job with fire. In harmonious chorus, antiseptic novels and schoolbooks like the pervasive McGuffey's *Readers* *(pages 98–99)* sang of the rewards of virtuous behavior, warning that lazy children would come to no good end.

But as soon as the class—or dinner or chores or whipping—was over, the kids nodded their heads, promise to be good, and then raced around the corner into their own private domain. There they were self-reliant, and could fashion their own brand of happiness with nothing more than a dog or a pocketknife, or a doll and some paints. Over the course of a year, games ebbed and flowed in a mystical, unbroken sequence. Kites, for example, might be popular for a week. Then kites would vanish and mumblety-peg or roller skates or kick-the-can or stilt-walking took over. Competition was often fierce and, in some games, the stakes were formidably high: if kids were playing "keepers" in marbles, a lost agate might set back the loser as much as 50 cents—more than a month's allowance.

But as the decade progressed, this rigid code and its underlying doctrine of self-reliance was no longer as necessary or as easy to uphold as it had been. Grownups moved in—for better or for worse—on the kids' world in ways they never had before. Daniel Beard, author of the wildly popular *American Boys Handy Book* (how to conduct snowball warfare, etc.), helped found the Boy Scouts in 1910. Publishing czar William Randolph Hearst made popular a new kind of kids' reading matter called the comic strip *(pages 92–93)*. Baseball cards, like those at right, were issued by cigarette companies in their packages as a sly bid for kids' attention. A collector's dream set would have 522 cards, but might not include the legendary shortstop Honus Wagner, whose picture had to be bootlegged by the tobacco companies since he refused to pose on grounds that he did not want to encourage youngsters to smoke.

" 'Penrod, what excuse have you to offer before I report your case to the principal?' The word 'principal' struck him in the vitals. Grand Inquisitor, Grand Khan, Sultan, Emperor, Tsar, Caesar Augustus— these are comparable."

Penrod, by Booth Tarkington

SCHAEFER, WASHINGTON

MATHEWSON, N. Y. NAT'L

CUBS

Joe Tinker OF THE CHICAGO NATIONALS

EVERS, CHICAGO NAT'L

CUBS

Frank L Chance OF THE CHICAGO NATIONALS

CLEVELAND

LAJOIE, CLEVELAND

KEELER, N. Y. AMER.

WHITE SOX

WALSH CHIC. AMER.

COBB, DETROIT

NAPS

YOUNG CLEVELAND AMER.

JENNINGS, DETROIT

BENDER, PHILA. AMER.

PIRATES

Fred L. Clarke OF THE PITTSBURG NATIONALS

M. BROWN, CHICAGO NAT'L

DELEHANTY, WASHINGTON

The Captain and the Kids

Spokesmen for Mischief

The Sunday funnies made a colorful entrance on the American scene on October 18, 1896, when the *New York Journal* published what it termed "eight pages of iridescent polychromous effulgence that makes the rainbow look like a lead pipe." Comic strips were an instant success and became daily features. The violent humor of the first funnies (one cartoon character performed such antics as breaking the jaw of a black boy and laughing merrily) was tempered to accommodate protesting parents. Pranks and embarrassing blunders became staple fare in *Happy Hooligan* and *The Captain and the Kids*, and happy animal drawings *(opposite, bottom)* decorated the funnies page. For the first time, kids were finding something in the newspapers that reflected their own love of deviltry. When Buster Brown and his dog Tige arrived in 1902 in a strip *(right)* that idealized mischief behind a thin veil of sermonizing, it expressed kids' feelings about themselves so perfectly that thousands of boys and dogs across the nation were soon sporting the nicknames of Buster and Tige.

Though a Buster Brown strip usually concluded with a parent-friendly moral, its spirit of mischievousness was the source of its enduring appeal to America's kids.

The dime-store novels were filled with plucky heroes, invariably able to overcome an array of treacherous circumstances with little more than stout-hearted virtue and unshakable courage.

The Ten-Cent Heroes

Hidden behind many a geography book full of dull facts about a country called Asia or something, there lurked a suspiciously ungeographical magazine. In the classroom, at friends' houses, almost anywhere away from the disapproving eyes of adults, boys turned to their favorite form of written fantasy, the dime novel—really a long short story bound into a five- or ten-cent magazine like those shown at left. The heroes who sprang from these pages—Fred Fearnot, Nick Carter, Bowery Billy—were personifications of the American ideal: pure of heart, doggedly ambitious and brave beyond belief.

The greatest of all dime-novel heroes was Frank Merriwell *(pages 96–97),* created for *Tip Top Weekly* by George Patten, alias Burt L. Standish. Patten wrote some 20,000 words a week and reached 125 million readers, but his writerly virtue had to be its own reward, for he received a maximum of $150 per issue, and died in poverty.

His fictional creation had a far better time of it. Frank Merriwell, in fact, could do no wrong. As Patten wrote, "His handsome proportions, his graceful, muscular figure, his fine, kingly head and that look of clean manliness . . . stamped him as a fellow of lofty thoughts and ambitions." First at Fardale Academy, then at Yale College, and later during worldwide adventures, the magnetic Frank Merriwell accomplished every task with perfect ease. Time and time again, he won the day in boxing, baseball (he possessed a pitch that curved in two directions), football, hockey, lacrosse, crew, track, shooting, bicycle racing, billiards, and golf. He outwitted Chinese bandits, Texas rustlers, and urban thugs. In addition to his feats of brain and muscle, he was good. When classmates stole a turkey from a farmer as a prank, Frank stayed behind to pin a five-dollar bill to the roost. He loved his mother, his alma mater, and his country; he abhorred poor sportsmanship, drinking, and bullies. The creator of this paragon of virtue once said, "I confess that my imagination was often pumped pretty dry," but for 20 years, he turned out such thrilling episodes as the one on the following page.

An Average Day for Frank

During one spring season Frank Merriwell was so busy starring on the baseball team and bidding for top place in his Yale class that he had no time for track. So he trained his friend Bart Hodge to run against Hood of Harvard in the mile event of the intercollegiate track meet. Unfortunately, Bart sprained his ankle at the very last moment, but he decided to run anyway.

"Then, just when it seemed that defeat was certain, he literally flung himself forward with a last burst of speed, passed the side of the Harvard runner, breasted the tape and plunged into the arms of Bart Hodge."

Frank Merriwell's Great Victory by George Patten

Preparations were being made for the mile run. Bart joined the starters. Then, at the last moment before the men were called to the mark, a great mad roar went up from the Yale stand. "Merriwell! Merriwell! Merriwell!"

Frank Merriwell was seen running across the field. "On your mark!" cried the starter. The men leaned forward on the line. "Set!" There was a straining of muscles. The runners crouched like human wolves ready for the spring.

Bang! Away they went. Frank Merriwell had reached the field in time to take his place as the substitute of Bart Hodge. He shot off from the mark with Dalton of Columbia at his shoulder.

Merriwell had counted on taking his pace from Hood, and he was disappointed when the man permitted Fealing of Georgetown and Dalton of Columbia to draw away. His disappointment increased as still others took the lead.

It occurred to him that Hood was playing a crafty trick. He was willing to sacrifice himself in order that Harvard might come out ahead of Yale. In order for Yale to take the lead she must win this event, while Harvard could lose it and still be at the top by a small margin.

At the half Frank gradually increased his speed. Old coaches looked on in consternation as they saw Frank pass man after man in that quarter. It seemed that he had made his burst too soon.

Now Merriwell felt the terrible strain, and he realized that Hood had used him to set the pace.

"Tricked!" groaned a Yale coach. "Merriwell can't keep it up to the tape!"

Now Hood was pressing Frank, who began to feel that he could not carry out the mighty task, yet who would not give his body the least relaxing. Every muscle of that splendid frame was tense, every nerve was strained. Frank's face was white as chalk. Once he seemed to reel. In that moment Hood reached his side and took the lead by 26 inches.

A cloudlike mist fluttered before Frank Merriwell's eyes. He knew that Hood had passed him. Through the cloud he saw grotesquely dancing figures beyond the finish. But his ears were deaf from the wild yells of the thousands.

"Come on, Merriwell—come on!"

"Hood wins!" roared the Crimson. "Har-vard! Har-vard!"

Frank knew the finish must be near. He gathered himself for the effort of his life. Then, just when it seemed that defeat was certain, he literally flung himself forward with a last burst of speed, passed the side of the Harvard runner, breasted the tape and plunged into the arms of Bart Hodge.

He had dropped, and like a mighty Niagara rose the roar that greeted the victor, for Merriwell had won at the last moment, and Yale was in the lead.

Roar! Roar! Roar! It went up to the blue sky! Men hugged each other, pounded each other, shrieked, danced and also died with joy.

"Merriwell!" roared the throng. "Merriwell! Merriwell!"

TipTop Weekly

An ideal publication for the American Youth

Issued Weekly. By Subscription $2.50 per year. Entered as Second Class Matter at New York Post Office by STREET & SMITH, 238 William St., N. Y.

No. 269.   **Price. Five Cents.**

FRANK MERRIWELL'S GREAT VICTORY

OR THE EFFORT OF HIS LIFE

BY BURT L. STANDISH

FRANK LITERALLY FLUNG HIMSELF FORWARD WITH A LAST GREAT BURST OF SPEED, BREASTED THE TAPE, AND PLUNGED INTO THE ARMS OF BART HODGE.

Dear Old Golden Rule Days

School, that unavoidable misfortune which befell all freedom-loving kids, offered a rather somber introduction to the world of books. While in some urban schools children were beginning to learn by doing things themselves *(left)*, millions of youngsters still cut their reading teeth on a five-book series known as McGuffey's *Readers,* containing short tales *(below),* verses, pronunciation and spelling lessons, and an anthology of English and American literature. Written in the 1830s and 1840s by a university professor named William Holmes McGuffey, they remained the literary staple for countless schools well into the 20th century. McGuffey grew up on a farm in Ohio and his *Readers* were successful because in an America still predominantly rural they spoke the language of rural children.

As soon as Jack found there were oranges in the baskets, he determined to have one, and going up to the basket, he slipped in his hand and took out one of the largest, and was making off with it.

But Charles said, Jack, you shall not steal these oranges while I have the care of them, and so you may just put that one back into the basket.

Not I, said Jack, as I am the largest, I shall do as I please; but Charles was not afraid, and taking the orange out of his hand, he threw it back into the basket.

Jack then attempted to go around to the other side and take one from the other basket; but as he stepped too near the horse's heels, he received a violent kick, which sent him sprawling to the ground.

His cries soon brought out the people from the house, and when they learned what had happened, they said that Jack was rightly served; and the orange man, taking Charles' hat, filled it with oranges, as he said he had been so faithful in guarding them, he should have all these for honesty.

Youthful investigators, urged on by a rather heavy-handed message from the blackboard, tackle the Eskimo Housing Question during a 1904 geography lesson.

An oddly assorted but dutiful public-school orchestra, with a barefoot cello player in the front row, tunes up at the first schoolhouse in St. Petersburg, Florida.

The Good Old Summertime

A pair of young straw-hatted friends, hand-in-hand, watch the receding tide of the Pacific.

"Summer afternoon—summer afternoon; to me those have always been the two most beautiful words in the English language."

Henry James, as quoted by Edith Wharton

Caught in the carefree mood of the summer season, a group of playful youngsters grins impishly from the middle of a haystack in a field in Pawling, New York.

There's nothing like the good old summer time," mused the songwriter and vaudeville star George "Honey Boy" Evans in 1902, during an alfresco luncheon with fellow musicians at Brighton Beach, in Brooklyn, New York. Apparently the rest of the nation agreed; Evans's casual remark, given a lilting melody and a set of lyrics, became one of the most popular songs of the decade.

There was no doubt, in fact, that summer was the season people loved best. For children it conjured up images of Fourth of July parades, baseball games, a favorite swimming hole or a romp in a haystack *(right)*. For their parents, it meant carefree outings in the countryside, excursions to trolley parks, perhaps a trip to one of the decade's "World's Fairs," and, most important of all, a chance to take part in a brand new American institution—the two-week summer vacation.

With the first warm weather, thousands of Americans began a migration to resort hotels in the mountains or at the seashore. Though accommodations were often cramped, the vacationers' mood was as expansive and carefree as the ocean itself. "Everything goes in summer," was the popular phrase, despite the cautionary advice of a popular etiquette book that "promiscuous intimacies at summer resorts are a great mistake!"

Many summer watering spots were decidedly honky-tonk. "Atlantic City," said *Cosmopolitan,* "is the eighth wonder of the world. It is overwhelming in its crudeness." Lining its sandy beach was "a lunatic's dream of peep-shows, cigar shops, merry-go-rounds, hotels, bazaars, fortune tellers' booths [and] seven miles of board walk crowded with 40,000 human beings."

For those who could not travel, the same sort of carnival excitement could be found at trolley parks near the edges of almost every large city. Built by streetcar companies to attract fares, these gaudy establishments, with their Ferris wheels, band concerts, baseball games, vaudeville acts, and boating ponds, offered both recreation and relief from the oppressive heat of the city. Half the fun, it seemed, was getting there—the pleasure of the cooling breeze produced by the speeding trolley car on its way to the park.

But despite its thrills and excitements, the real pleasures of summer were the simple ones—the chance to get out of doors, to stroll down a tree-shaded lane, and to experience the general feeling that times were good and life in America was indeed worth living.

The Old Hometown

QUIET PATIENCE ON THE PRAIRIE

Main Street in Dorrance, Kansas, as seen from the town's water tower, snakes off into prairie.

Life in a Prairie Town

Patience was a way of life for at least 45 million Americans at the turn of the century. Those millions, comprising the 60 percent of the population that resided in towns of fewer than 2,500 people, endured as country folk always had, in the grip of the seasons, following the rhythm of planting and harvesting. So it was for the wheatgrowers of Dorrance, an austere little town huddled on a windy prairie in north-central Kansas.

During its half-century of existence, Dorrance had never been more than a speck on the map, but it had seen a lot of history. The area had been crossed by Indian hunters, by wagon trains of settlers, and by gold seekers. In 1867, the Union Pacific Railroad tracks reached Dorrance, bringing with them the German, Irish, and other immigrants who accounted for much of the town's modest growth after 1870. By 1910, when Dorrance was incorporated, it had only 281 citizens, yet it was one of the most important towns in Russell County.

Not without cause, the townspeople took quiet pride in their community. Dorrance had everything a country town really needed: a good public school, with four teachers and about 100 pupils; a bank and a hotel; four churches; a variety of stores and businesses; telephone and telegraph service. This was a progressive town. Decades earlier, farmers had built windmills that still pumped their water. Recently a few men had acquired modern steam-driven threshers, and the Mahoney family even bought a car when autos were still a novelty in the cities.

The people themselves, shown here in pictures taken by Leslie Halbe, the banker's son, were exactly what their town suggested: a plain, durable folk who feared God and worked hard. In their need for relief from the prairie's raw isolation, people drew together and got on well. German and Frenchman, Catholic and Mennonite pitched in to help one another at harvest time and to outfit the town's baseball team. No one got rich, but no one was poor.

In such small towns life had a continuity that extended beyond the grave. The dead, buried in cemeteries inside the town, were as much a part of Dorrance as the blacksmith's shop and Weber's lumberyard; their graves were visited on Decoration Day by all the citizens, led by Civil War veterans in faded uniforms. Few people, living or dead, left Dorrance; almost everyone stayed on, content and patient to labor and to wait.

> "This town is the fruit of great aspiration, and we who live here now have a debt to posterity that we can pay only by still achieving, still pursuing; we must learn to labor and to wait."
>
> William Allen White, editor of the Emporia, Kansas, *Gazette*

Dorrance's station crew waits for a train under a sign listing distances to the nearest big cities. Here salesmen detrained and hawked their wares for miles around.

Two landmarks on Main Street, the post office and village drugstore, were built of limestone from nearby quarries and lumber that had to be brought in by rail.

Dorrance's telephone switchboard operator had few calls and plenty of time to chat. Twice she had no work when blizzards knocked down all the wires.

The Citizens' State Bank issued loans to families between harvests. One major cause for seasonal borrowing was the average farmer's need for a dozen work horses.

Town workers and visitors on business are served family style by a dexterous short-order cook in Sheetz's Restaurant on Main Street.

Wearing their Sunday suits, two young farmers, Peter Steinle and Henry Heinze, share a buggy ride to Dorrance from their outlying spread.

The Lutheran Church lets out its congregation, about 60 families strong. Dorrance had three other denominations, all with white frame churches of their own.

*A wheatgrower unloads his crop at a grain elevator.
This elevator was constructed by German immigrants
who brought with them the winter wheat grown locally.*

A farmer sets out from the John Deere dealership with a new header machine to reap his wheat. Harvesting began in July and took about 12 days.

A man identified as S. Shilts tended pigs to supplement the income from his wheat crop. A typical local farmer, he cultivated about 300 acres of land.

At harvest time, a wheat farmer's family gathers together on the water wagon, which was driven out to refill the steam engine that powered the threshing machine.

Emerging Women

★

HOME, ROMANCE, INDEPENDENCE

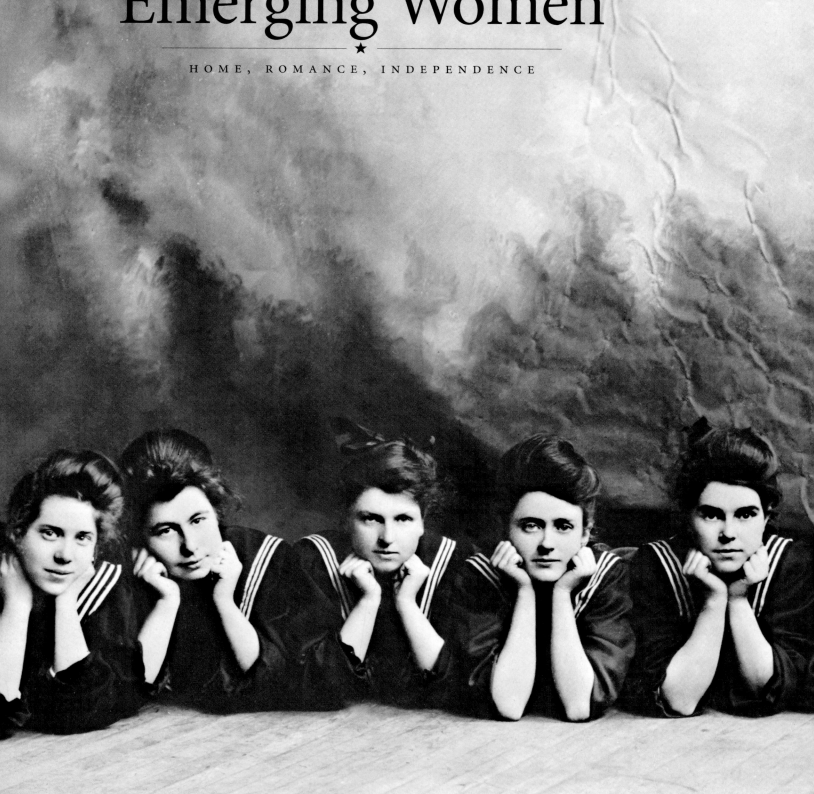

A girls' basketball squad, evidence of the more active life women found in the new century, poses for the team picture.

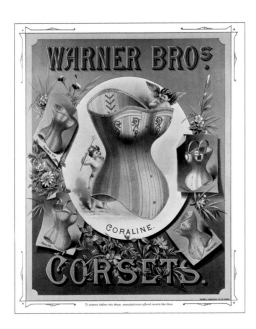

"In other countries you may be gently urged for an appreciation of the architecture of galleries; but the American man will, in nine cases out of ten, make his first question of the visiting foreigner—"Well, what do you think of our women?"

Katherine G. Busbey, writer, 1910

Anna Held, the coquettish French star of musical comedy, was once accused by a blue-nosed critic of causing sexual unrest with her lovely legs and 18-inch waist.

A Woman's Place

When George Bernard Shaw was asked his opinion of American women in 1907, he responded with this burst of misogyny: "Every American woman explains that she is an absolute exception and is not like any other American woman. But they are all exactly the same. The only thing to be said for them is they are usually very well dressed and extraordinarily good looking." That was exactly the way unenlightened American men wanted their women: beautiful, but not so bright and sassy that they wandered from their place in the home.

The emancipation of women from male domination—as well as from fanciful costumes requiring steel-reinforced corsets *(left)* and a life close to the hearth—was barely beginning as the century dawned. Fully one quarter of the states then in the Union denied a married woman the right to own property; one third of them allowed her no claim on her own earnings—even if she worked to support a shiftless husband. And 36 of them, or four-fifths, denied her an equal share in the guardianship of her children.

Of course most men, defenders of the status quo that they were, refused to see the inequity in this. Despite their lack of legal rights, the men argued, women had many compensations. "They haven't th' right to vote," conceded Mr. Dooley, the fictitious philosopher created by humorist Finley Peter Dunne, "but they have th' priv'lege iv controllin' th' man ye ilict. They haven't th' right to make laws, but they have th' priv'lege iv breakin' thim, which is betther. They haven't the right iv a fair thrile be a jury iv their peers; but they have th' priv'lege iv an unfair thrile be a jury iv their admirin' infeeryors. If I cud fly d'ye think I'd want to walk?"

Women, so went the prevailing masculine wisdom, need not bother themselves with political rights; better they should get their way by dazzling their menfolk with so-called "feminine wiles." In this course they were abetted by a flood of "women's literature"—romantic fiction that created an ideal of the softly genteel but indomitable female, and magazines that gave them how-to instructions for achieving the ideal. Articles preached decorum and cautioned against dangerous new ideas. *Vogue* warned in 1900, "All decent people are agreed that the emancipated novelists are not fit reading," and listed as taboo the "cancerous literature" of Ibsen, Zola, and Shaw among others. Along with such admonitions went a steady stream of advice on beauty and fashion, which, according to the

1. Toque with satin bow, advertised as
suitable for morning
2. Tailored toque with velvet brim, silk crown and bow
3. Evening hat in flowered silk and plaited chiffon
4. Afternoon hat with egret plume and
satin-faced brim
5. Evening hat in velvet and silk, made "for
a blonde"
6. Picture hat in two-toned velvet and chiffon

3   4   5   6

acid Shaw, was American women's most obvious asset.

Women adorned themselves with clothes of great variety and elegance, and they spent an unparalleled amount of money doing it: over a billion dollars a year, $14 million of it on corsets alone. The crowning glory of a proper lady's get-up was her hat, and many women never set foot outdoors without one. It was usually liberally garnished with poufs of lace, yards of ribbon, bouquets of flowers, bunches of fruit—and besides any or all of these, it frequently carried a nest of birds.

So prodigal was the slaughter of birds to appease the gods of women's fashion that at a single monthly auction in London in 1900 the plumage of more than 24,000 egrets was up for sale—a fact that the Audubon Society protested in vain. In 1905 the Sears, Roebuck catalog devoted most of a page to some 75 versions of ostrich feathers for women's headgear; and if ostriches were not to the lady's taste, she could adorn her hats instead with clusters of purple grackles or red-winged blackbirds, ori-

oles or skylarks, pigeons or doves, thrushes or wrens—in short, with almost anything that once had chirped.

Below her fancy bonnets a lady wore equally elaborate dresses like those *(next page)* that were illustrated in 1906 in a magazine with the classy Frenchified title of *L'Art de la Mode and le Charme United*. Generally she made them herself—or had a dressmaker fashion them for her —from McCall or Butterick patterns; but mass-manufactured clothes were coming on the market as immigrant Jewish tailors poured in from pogrom-ridden Poland and Russia. "There is no place in the world where such dainty machine-made garments of all sorts can be found as in American department stores," wrote Katherine G. Busbey. The American innovation of well-made ready-to-wear clothes was accompanied by a notable native contribution to fashion: the shirtwaist, a blouse meant to be worn with a skirt. Paris couture looked down its nose on this aberration, but American women paid no heed. They first took to the shirtwaist in the 1890s. By

1905 the Sears, Roebuck catalog was offering 150 different versions of it, from a plain one in lawn at 39 cents to a grand concoction in taffeta at $6.95. In 1907 came the peek-a-boo shirtwaist, a daring creation of eyelet embroidery that allowed the flesh of a lady's arms to show. By 1910 the national production of shirtwaists was big business; New York alone turned out 60 million dollars' worth.

The skirts with which the ladies wore their shirtwaists were generally long, but once in a while they rakishly bared an ankle. In 1905 Sears, Roebuck, never a firm to be in the vanguard, offered "Ladies' Walking Skirts"—garments that "are made expressly for convenience and are also known as the Health Skirt."

Shirtwaists and shorter skirts were more than fashion whims. Simpler clothing, easier to wear and more suitable to an active life, was demanded by the new and freer role that women had begun to seek. In increasing numbers they were going out into the world, taking jobs in offices, shops and factories. The feminist movement, agitating vigorously for legal rights, swept many women into political activity. But public life and outside work were adventures for only a daring minority and for poor, African-American or immigrant women whose economic circumstances demanded that they contribute to the family income. The average middle-class woman concerned herself with a traditional role—obliging her husband, rearing her children, making her nest a cozy place, easing her cares with light reading. The woman's place was still in the home.

---

1. *Princess gown in green chiffon velvet pressed to look like ribbing*
2. *Eton suit in blue broadcloth trimmed with folds of matching velvet*
3. *Evening gown of peach satin trimmed with lace and velvet ribbon*
4. *Indoor dress in London smoke cloth with embroidered silk braid*
5. *Gown of primrose faille, with white satin collar, cuffs; black satin revers*

2   3   4   5

The Rosy World of Romance

Just as every American man knew at the turn of the century that with hard work he was bound to get ahead, so every woman took it on faith that love conquered all. If life failed to bear her out, there was a reassuring flood of romantic fiction from magazines whose saccharine covers *(right)*—with stories to match—kept the ladies' eyes fixed on a world beyond the workaday kitchen. The following passage is condensed from a serial in *The Delineator*. The story, like others of its kind, was full of mini-tragedies. But the sensitive reader may be assured that in the final installment the dashing suitor will return to save the heroine from a life without love.

"She tried to withdraw the rash admission, startled by the rapture in his face, but could not, for Stelvio's arms were around her, he was kissing her face and hair."

The Delineator

With his sinuous hands on her satin flesh, a lover gives his paramour—and the stay-at-home with her magazine—a taste of true romance.

It was all over with her past; her brief passionate love dream was forever put aside! Never a word had come from Stelvio since the witching night on the Grand Canal in Venice.

Now back at home in Virginia she wandered like a soul in pain, and finally one evening stole out to an old favorite spot of childhood, a hillock in the nearby forest massed with wild blossoms from Spring to Autumn. Here Margot dropped upon a bench, and for the last time, so she told herself, lived over the hour in Far Niente garden when she gave her heart away never to be recalled. She would soon be McPhail's wife, since to him her poor family must look for support.

Stelvio! Oh! for a last word with him to ease her bursting heart. One look only!

And here, through the thick underwood came to her, in answer to this cry of the heart, Stelvio in person, pale, haggard, worn, deep love and reproach in his eyes!

"You? You here?" she cried. "Oh! it can't be!"

Then his words came in an impetuous, fiery stream.

"I am here because I heard you were soon to marry. When Countess Fleury told me this was so I went away from home and sailed directly for America. Margot, I cannot bear it; I can't lose you; I can't let that vulgar brute take from me all my treasures. If I did not believe you love me, me only, if you can look me in the eyes and say you don't, why I will give up and go away, crushed and beaten. But I won't do it without trying to keep you. That night I sang to you in Venice, I knew my voice went straight to your heart and when no word came, when silence fell between us like a black veil, I was sore and wounded, but had no thought of change."

"And you supposed you've had all the sorrow?" cried she, hotly. "You make nothing of my suffering."

She tried to withdraw the rash admission, startled by the rapture in his face, but could not, for Stelvio's arms were around her, he was kissing her face and hair.

"Ah! Don't struggle, Margot dearest, don't put me away, when your words, your eyes, everything, confess your love for me," he cried. "Speak! Answer me! Tell me that you are mine, mine, mine!"

For one brief moment she had answered his heartbeats with her own and exultingly let him hold her close. Yet she was enabled to stand firm by the promptings of her spirit.

"Margot, forgive me. I am a brute to torture you. God knows if I could save you from this fate without thought of myself and my own longing for you, I'd do so—"

"You can't, you can't," she exclaimed mournfully. "But we were happy, weren't we?" she went on, plaintively.

He understood her. All his being thrilled in answer to these sweet avowals, but he made no move to approach her.

She stood gazing after him until he struck into the highroad. Then she could see him no more for bitter, blinding tears.

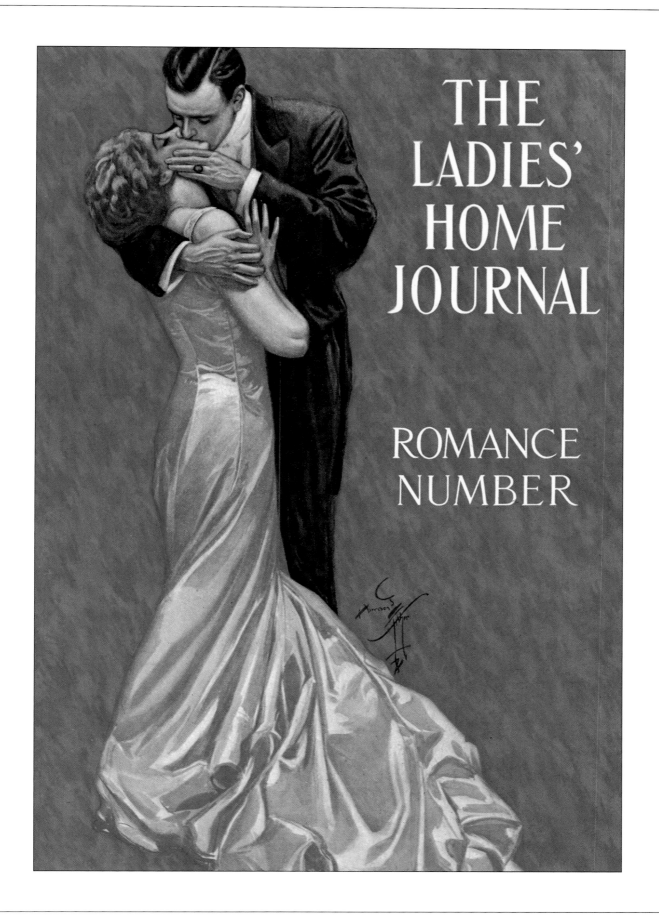

A House from the Wish Book

For most young American women, the rosy dreams implanted by romantic reading faded as they grew up. After they married, they almost inevitably found themselves confined to the home, but to a home that was changing rapidly. Even in the country, women were acquiring labor-saving devices for their kitchens, fancy gewgaws for their parlors, and sometimes well-equipped boudoirs for themselves. They were able to do so largely due to a new way of buying the things they had read about in their magazines and books. Now they could order practically whatever they wanted out of a mail-order catalog, no matter how far they might live from the tantalizing stores of a big city.

This revolutionary merchandising idea was conceived by Aaron Montgomery Ward in 1872, but Richard W. Sears, a onetime railroad clerk, and A. C. Roebuck, a watchmaker, perfected it. Their modest jewelry shop, founded in 1887, became a wondrous emporium that supplied housewives from Maine to California with every conceivable kind of merchandise.

The catalog—much of which was written by Sears himself—was fondly known to American women and their families as the "wish book." For the kitchen, it offered fancy stoves with embossed nickel trimmings, iceboxes that made possible the safe storage of perishables, and an ice-cream freezer that was "miles in advance of any other make." Its parlor fittings included musical instruments—pianos, organs, banjos and guitars—then deemed essential for the proper home. For the lady's boudoir, Sears offered, along with such beauty aids as combs, perfumes and curling irons, a pharmacopeia of patent medicines, many of them of highly questionable value.

In the winter of 1904–1905 the traffic in worthless nostrums came under heavy fire when Edward Bok, the formidable editor of the *Ladies' Home Journal,* ran a series of exposés in his magazine. *Collier's Weekly* followed the next winter, and Congress came to the public's rescue by passing the Pure Food and Drugs Act, which required that drugs meet certain standards and advertising rid itself of spurious claims. Honest firms quickly fell in line, and by 1909 the Sears catalog carried nothing more potent than epsom salts and aspirin in its drug department. An era of naiveté and simplicity was coming to a close, and Sears, whose wish book had helped to bring the outside world into the American home, was speeding the process.

The real heroine of the first decade lived not in romantic fiction but in the American kitchen (opposite); and she, too, had her hero—Sears, Roebuck & Co. and its handy catalog (above).

Wood-burning stove $17.48

Bread toaster 20¢

Ice cream freezer $1.26

Snap-on handle and three irons 75¢

Cherry stoner 70¢

Wooden icebox $8.92

Coffee grinder 49¢

Enameled teapot 58¢

1 oz. perfume, any scent 40¢

China, part of 10-piece set $2.59

4½-inch shell hairpins 4¢ each

Hair-waving iron 11¢

Female pills 33¢

Hatpins 5¢ each

2-oz. jar of bust cream 40¢

Cold cream 28¢

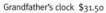

Rope portiere $3.98

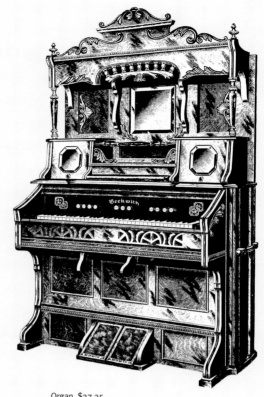

Grandfather's clock $31.50

Oak extension table $13.95

Organ $37.35

Manicure and toilet set $1.69

Perfume atomizer 37¢

Turkish leather couch $15.65

All-purpose hair tonic 57¢

Pompadour comb 29¢

Turkish leather rocker $32.75

Deluxe talking machine $45

Four "lady typewriters" take the air at lunchtime. In most offices working women were permitted only 15 to 30 minutes for midday larks.

Women Leave Home

Though most women were content to play the traditional role of keeper of the home, a growing band of determined rebels was leading a march away from the pots and pans and into the exciting, man-filled world beyond. They quickly made themselves indispensable to industry and a force to be reckoned with in public affairs. At first blush the men seemed to think this invasion of male precincts was dreadful. "Men want a girl," huffed *Independent* magazine in April 1901, "who has not rubbed off the peach blossom of innocence by exposure to a rough world." Whether or not the men professed to like women in their new roles, the truth was that the men needed them there.

In business offices, the bursting growth of the American economy had created an avalanche of paperwork. A wonderful contraption called the typewriter had been invented to speed letter writing. However, male clerks found the machine a bore to operate and refused to have any truck with it. So women tried the new machine and from then on the doors to business life were open to them. Whereas in 1870 there had been but seven women stenographers in all of America, by 1900 there were more than 100,000 "lady typewriters."

The attractions of a business job were more than simply money—though that was no small consideration, since in an office a woman could make $10 or more a week, twice what she could earn in a kitchen or an old-fashioned sweatshop. There was also for some the

A young lady named Marcella (above) beams with pride in her job away from home—bookkeeping at the Standard Lime & Stone Co. in Fond du Lac, Wisconsin.

attraction of meeting a potential husband, even if in order to find the right man one was forced to deal with mashers like the thugs portrayed in self-defense manuals *(right)*.

The working woman was not the only one who was itching to get out of the house. Her married sister was ready, too. And with no end of handy gadgets from the Sears wish book to speed her kitchen chores, she had more time to get around than her mother had had. The first thing she usually did was join a woman's club, one of those earnest organizations dedicated to helping the poor—or simply to providing for the "self-improvement" of the members themselves.

By the end of the decade, almost a million women belonged to such groups. Some pressured local governments to create juvenile courts; others brought about enlightened child-labor laws; still others were little more than glorified social clubs. As the movement continued to grow, it sometimes drew the ire of reform-minded—and perhaps somewhat sexist—men such as Edward Bok, the powerful editor of the *Ladies' Home Journal,* who fired off a blast *(condensed below)* in his January 1910 issue.

Now what has the average woman's club done during the past five years? What has the average woman's club done for clearer understanding of self-sex and life in the mind of the child? Absolutely nothing. What has the average woman's club done to agitate or prevent the needless blindness of 33 percent of little blind babies? What has been done by the average woman's club toward the curse that is the one direct cause of sending 80 percent of the women of today to the operating table? What has the average woman's club done toward the abolishment of the public drinking cup? What has the average woman's club done toward the repression in newspapers of indecent advertisements relating to private diseases, nostrums, dangerous "beauty" remedies for the skin and hair?

Until the woman's club shall show a more intelligent conception of its trusteeship, I insist that the woman's club up to date has been "weighed in the balance and found wanting."

A threatened woman (right, top) wields her umbrella against a masher, deftly "stopping a blow aimed at the face" and jabbing the ruffian's jaw.

Reinforced by a sprinkling of male auxiliaries, the Royal Neighbors of America line up in their Kansas clubhouse for a display of uniforms, spears and banners.

The Gibson Girl

From 1890 until the First World War, American women between the ages of 15 and 30 yearned to be like the dazzling visions that floated through the ink drawings of Charles Dana Gibson. The Gibson girl—tall and stately, superbly dressed, artful but never truly wicked—first appeared in illustrations in the old humor magazine *Life*. Overnight she became the idol and the model for a generation.

"Before Gibson synthesized his ideal woman, the American girl was vague, nondescript, inchoate," wrote a reporter in the New York *World*. "As soon as the world saw Gibson's ideal it bowed down in adoration, saying: 'Lo, at last the typical American girl.'"

The adulation paid his pen-and-ink ladies astonished Gibson, who regarded himself as a social and political satirist, not as a style-setter for women. "If I hadn't seen it in the papers," he said, "I should never have known that there was such a thing as a Gibson girl."

He was, apparently, the only one in such ignorance. So eagerly did women look to his paragon for arbitrament in fashion that Gibson was charged with competing against the famous Butterick dress patterns, and one contemporary observer wrote: "You can always tell when a girl is taking the Gibson Cure by the way she fixes her hair."

Men were just as smitten with the Gibson girl; imitating the handsome swains who always attended her, they shaved their mustaches and padded the shoulders of their jackets. And more than one carefree blade decorated his living quarters with Gibson girl wallpaper, which the manufacturer touted as just the thing for a bachelor apartment.

Gibson amiably granted licenses to put his girls on china plates, silverware, dresser sets, pillows, whiskbroom holders, and virtually any other respectable surface that would accommodate them. But when an automobile manufacturer asked him to enter an advertising contest, offering a cash prize if he won but demanding the right to keep the drawing if he lost, he retorted: "I am running a competition for automobiles. Kindly submit one of yours. If acceptable, it wins an award. If rejected, it becomes my property."

Gibson used an abundance of this kind of waspish wit, together with his talent for drawing unsurpassable girls, to poke fun at the foibles of society—in fiction illustrations, in cartoons, and in serialized picture stories that the artist captioned himself.

The eyes of magazine illustrator Charles Dana Gibson reflect the wit that sparked his drawings.

The ideal American girl as seen by her creator was chic, haughty, graceful, and above all else, shatteringly pretty.

Woman of the Decade

Though the ladies of the first decade may have held differing views on the proper role of the American woman, they had before them a living example of the girl they would all have liked to be. She was Alice Roosevelt, daughter of Teddy—who was himself the man of the decade. Alice Roosevelt was 17 when her father entered the

> **"I can do one of two things. I can be President of the United States, or I can control Alice. I cannot possibly do both."**
>
> Theodore Roosevelt

White House in late 1901, and before he left he confessed (*above*) to the immensity of the role he was asked to play. An exceptionally pretty girl, Alice (*right*) was the living embodiment of the Gibson girl, an artist's idealized concept of American womanhood. She was, moreover, every bit as spirited as her father. The newspapers delighted in calling her "a chip off the old block," and TR did not mind at all. With obvious relish he told a friend that Alice "does not stay in the house and fold her hands and do nothing."

Far from it. The *Journal des Débats* in Paris noted that in 15 months Alice Roosevelt had attended 407 dinners, 350 balls and 300 parties. She danced till dawn, "with the men who had least reason to expect the honor," observed one interested newsman, "and laughingly disappointed those who had counted on her."

All America was in love with her. Women named their babies Alice and dressed themselves up in Alice-blue gowns. Bands at horse races, rallies, and railroad stations greeted the president's daughter with a song played in her honor, "Alice, Where Art Thou?"

Everywhere she went, she airily flouted the stodgy conventions of the decade. She smoked openly—when well-bred ladies seldom smoked even in private. On shipboard she once jumped into a swimming pool fully dressed—and drew a congressman in behind her. In Washington she gave many a politician a run for his money at the poker table. In New York, when she found a party flagging at her Auntie Bye's, she fired a toy pistol into the air.

If she startled society, Alice Roosevelt enchanted the rest of America with the unabashed pleasure she took both in herself and in the perquisites of first family rank. She exulted in the gifts that foreign dignitaries showered on her—among them a little black dog from the empress of China and a diamond bracelet from the kaiser of Germany.

Europe hung on her doings as breathlessly as did America. The French magazine *Femina* ran her picture on the front page, together with pictures of Europe's eligible princes. The British government considered conferring royal status upon her (a proposal her father declined) so that she might attend the coronation of King Edward VII in Westminster Abbey without violating protocol. The Japanese lined the streets and shouted *Banzai!* when she visited Tokyo. The empress of China invited Alice to spend a night at the Imperial Palace in Peking. And the sultan of Sulu, who was four feet tall, was reported to have asked for the hand of the "American princess," whom he thought to add to his harem as wife number seven.

Like all good princesses, Alice was indeed married, though not to the sultan of Sulu. In 1905 she announced her engagement to an Ohio congressman, Nicholas Longworth, whom the Washington *Times* called "the national bridegroom." Her wedding, of course, was the smash of the season, the perfect climax to a brilliant adventure in American girlship that not even the most poised and stunning of Charles Dana Gibson's imaginary ladies ever truly matched.

The image of the Gibson girl–from the tilt of her pompadoured head to the fall of her filmy skirt–Alice Roosevelt sat for a photo when she lived in the White House.

Sports

ATHLETICS ATTRACT A FOLLOWING

The New York Athletic Club wrestling squad lines up for a show of muscle.

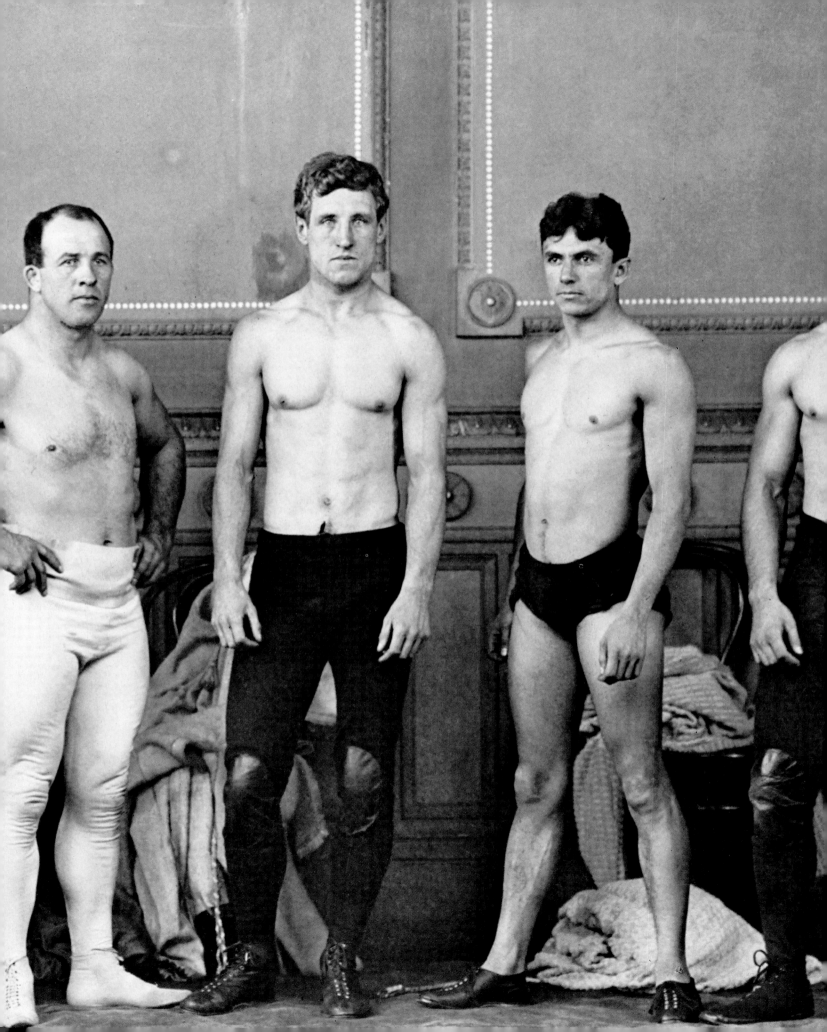

Brave Deeds by Some Bully Boys

"In life, as in a football game, the principle to follow is: hit the line hard; don't foul and don't shirk, but hit the line hard!"

Theodore Roosevelt

I

t was a bully time in American sport. Boxing fans flocked by the tens of thousands to witness fights such as the widely trumpeted "Battle of the Century" *(pages 148–149)* between the incomparable Jim Jeffries and the skillful black boxer Jack Johnson, whose ability to beat white fighters such as Jeffries offended racist sensibilities.

Baseball had truly gone big-time with the formation of a second major league called the American to rival the long-established National. Now children had twice the number of heroes to root for: Honus Wagner and Willie ("Hit 'em Where They Ain't") Keeler were joined by new idols like Chief Bender, the full-blooded Indian pitcher for the Philadelphia Athletics, and Tyrus Raymond Cobb, fiery center fielder of the Detroit Tigers.

Amateur sport had also become enormously popular. The first Olympics had come to the United States *(pages 146–147)*. College football, until recently a muddy sort of grunt-and-push amusement confined to a few Eastern colleges, had begun to blossom as a rival even to baseball. Chunky Willie Heston led the 1901–1904 Michigan squads of Coach Fielding H. "Hurry-up" Yost to such an awesome string of high-scoring victories that Michigan became known as the "point-a-minute" football team. Carlisle Indian School, a tiny school in Pennsylvania, fell heir to a remarkable athlete named Jim Thorpe, who single-handedly demolished such great powers as Army and Penn. Yet in this decade the premier football teams were still those of Harvard and Yale, whose gentleman halfbacks hit the line with a savagery that others found hard to match.

It was not that others did not try. By 1905 college and high school football had become so ferocious that 19 players were killed during the season. President Theodore Roosevelt, despite his exhortations about the virtues of bashing into the line, persuaded a group of college presidents to draw up a more humane code of rules. The result was a newer, more open game which Yale and Harvard quickly mastered. Undefeated through the seasons of '05, '06 and its first nine games of '07, Yale met a Harvard team that was also undefeated in '07. But Yale, sparked by the slashing runs of its halfbacks—and a new play called the forward pass, which completely baffled its opponent—swept to a 12–0 win in a game that Old Blues would swear was the finest athletic contest in history.

Lowering his tousled head, Yale's sophomore halfback Stephen Philbin barrels through a confusion of Harvard tacklers in a 1907 championship game.

A Wild First World Series

October 4, 1903—It was the greatest day in attendance the Boston Americans have ever known, more than 18,000 of the 25,000 being paid attendance. Swarming into the field, the eager thousands put ball playing temporarily out of the question. Finally Patrolman Louis Brown of Station 10 appeared with a long section of rubber hose. Using it partly as a rope, partly as a club, the police gradually drove back the human wall. Members of both nines were using their bats in much the same manner till finally the diamond and a mimic outfield had been cleared. Right here was where Boston lost the game before it was ever started. A ground rule was made whereby a hit into the crowd would be good for two bases. Before the third inning had been completed the visitors made four base hits, three of which should have been easy outs. The two runs resulting were the margin by which the home team lost.

October 14, 1903—Boston's American League team defeated Pittsburgh at the Huntington Avenue grounds yesterday and thereby won the world's championship. It was the eighth and decisive game, Boston winning five to Pittsburgh's three. Big Bill Dinneen shut the National League team out without a run. Hardly had the mighty Wagner closed the ninth inning with a third futile swing at Dinneen's elusive curves when a wild yell of triumph went up. The Boston Americans had vindicated the confidence of their supporters most nobly. While the grandstand swayed and rocked with the mighty salvos of applause, while Boston's players were borne by the fans in triumph to the dressing room, a dozen grey-clad Pittsburgh players, alone and almost unnoticed, walked slowly across the field and headed for the distant gate. Fallen champions they were, who had at last met their Waterloo in Boston.

Nasty Surprise for the Nationals

When a sportswriter named Byron Bancroft Johnson put together baseball's American League in 1900, the tradition-bound, tight-fisted leaders of the 24-year-old National League saw no threat to their hold on the game. But after three years of tense interleague warfare, in which the upstart Americans lured away fans and players, the Nationals gave up and sued for peace. On March 6, 1903, a code of Joint Playing Rules was signed and became the baseball law of the land. Better yet from the fans' point of view, six months later the Boston Pilgrims, champions of the new league, signed a contract to meet the National League–leading Pittsburgh team in a postseason series for the baseball championship of the world. The first World Series began on October 1 in Boston's Huntington Avenue grounds. The Pilgrims showed themselves equal to the challenge by polishing off the best-of-nine series in the eighth game. At left are excerpts from the partisan Boston *Post*, which reported the crowd's interference in the third game, and the victory in the eighth.

Pittsburgh's National League champions glumly watch from the dugout. Fourth from the left is Honus Wagner, the Pirates star who struck out to end the series.

Fans pour onto the field at Boston's Huntington Avenue Baseball Grounds after Pittsburgh's 4–2 win over Boston in game 3. The cheapest seat cost 50 cents, twice the amount charged for the season's regular games.

Olympian Confusion in St. Louis

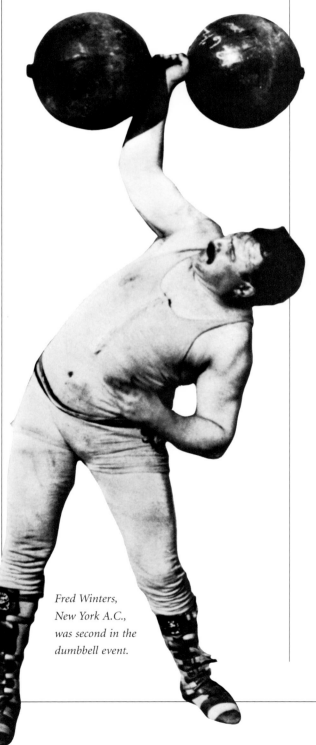

Fred Winters, New York A.C., was second in the dumbbell event.

The third Olympic Games, held as an adjunct to the St. Louis World's Fair of 1904, were more notable for their giddy confusion than for athletic virtuosity. Only six foreign countries showed up. As a result, the U.S. won 22 of the 23 track and field events. And the Games became a dogfight among the various athletic clubs that had sponsored the American competitors.

It also became a kind of athletic freak show. In a bizarre competition called Anthropology Days, a lead-footed American Indian won the 100-meter dash in 11.8 seconds with an African Pygmy bringing up the rear in 14.6. An Ainu from Japan threw the 56-pound hammer one yard and a few odd inches. That was the low point until Fred Lorz, apparent winner of the marathon, received his crown from none other than Presi-

dent Roosevelt's popular daughter Alice—then had it unceremoniously snatched away when a local truck driver confessed he had given Lorz a lift over the last part of the course.

The final indignity occurred when the New York Athletic Club eked out a second in the hammer throw and a fourth in the tug-of-war *(below)*, to score an overall Olympic victory—whereupon the second-place Chicago A.C. protested. That was too much for the St. Louis *Post-Dispatch*, and it roasted the loser in the editorial excerpted at right.

The tug-of-war (below), in which the stalwarts of the New York Athletic Club finished fourth, was the decisive event of the first Olympic Games held in the United States.

While 19,000 spectators were on their feet and cheering, the Chicago Athletic Association was protesting the four points by which the New York Athletic Club defeated them for the Olympic championship. The three points for John De Witt's second in the hammer throw were protested and the one point for fourth in the tug-of-war also was. The method of protest makes clear the underlying motive. The Chicago men were fairly beaten and to the undying shame of the Western country, a western organization has shown that it does not know how to take a beating.

"The Negro Showed No Yellow"

On July 4, 1910, Jim Jeffries came out of retirement to try to wrest the heavyweight boxing championship from Jack Johnson, the first black to hold that title. Bigoted Americans cheered for the defeat of the black swashbuckler who clearly did not know his place. Jack London *(inset)*—novelist and devout racist—recorded for the San Francisco *Chronicle*, with the headline above and story condensed at right, the country's surprise at the outcome.

> "The greatest battle of the century was a monologue delivered to twenty thousand spectators by a smiling Negro who was never in doubt and who was never serious for more than a moment at a time."
>
> Jack London

Johnson has sent down to defeat the chosen representative of the white race, and this time the greatest of them all. And, as of old, it was play for Johnson. From the opening to the closing round he never ceased his witty sallies, his exchange of repartee with his opponent's seconds and with the spectators. And, for that matter, Johnson had a funny thing or two to say to Jeffries in every round. The golden smile was as much in evidence as ever, and neither did it freeze on his face nor did it vanish.

Johnson played, as usual, blocking and defending in masterly fashion. And he played and fought a white man, in a white man's country before a white man's crowd. And the crowd was a Jeffries crowd. When Jeffries sent in that awful rip of his the crowd would madly applaud, believing it had gone home to Johnson's stomach, and Johnson, deftly interposing his elbow, would smile in irony at the spectators, play-acting, making believe he thought the applause was for him—and never believing it at all.

Great Battle a Monologue

The greatest battle of the century was a monologue delivered to twenty thousand spectators by a smiling Negro who was never in doubt and who was never serious for more than a moment at a time. Never once was he extended. No blow Jeff ever landed hurt his dusky opponent. Johnson came out of the great fight practically undamaged. The blood on his lip was from a recent cut received in training, which Jeff managed to reopen.

While Jeff was dead game to the end, he was not so badly punished. What he failed to bring into the ring with him was his stamina, which he lost somewhere in the last seven years. His old-time vim and endurance were not there. As I have said, Jeff was not badly damaged. Every day boys take worse beatings in boxing bouts than Jeff took today.

Jeff today disposed of one question. He could not come back. Johnson, in turn, answered another question. He has not the yellow streak. But he only answered that question for today. The ferocity of the hairy-chested caveman and grizzly giant combined did not intimidate the cool-headed Negro. Many thousands in the audience expected this intimidation and were correspondingly disappointed. Johnson was not scared, let it be said here and beyond the shadow of any doubt. Not for a second did he show the flicker of a fear at the Goliath against him.

Question of the Yellow Streak

But the question of the yellow streak is not answered for all time. Just as Johnson has never been extended, so has he never shown the yellow streak. Just as a man may rise up, heaven knows where, who will extend Johnson, just so may that man bring out the yellow streak, and then, again, he may not.

Jabbing and hooking, Johnson kept up a banter with ringsiders and taunted the floundering Jeffries during the fight: "Mister Jeff, you ain't showed me nothin' yet."

Two coaches pass on a tree-lined drive. Etiquette for such encounters was strict. On first meeting, one bowed; on second, one smiled; on third, one looked away.

The Very Rich

★

Heyday of the Big Spenders

"We are not rich. We have only a few million."

Mrs. Stuyvesant Fish

Miss Louise Scott (wearing flowered hat) and Mrs. Gordon Douglass enjoy a key activity of the very rich—observing and being observed—as they promenade on a Newport greensward.

Mrs. Stuyvesant Fish, long a leader of high society, had good cause to lament the meagerness of her fortune. At one opulent party, as she and Mr. Fish arose to depart early, a vulgar parvenu named Harry Lehr said arrogantly, "Sit down, Fishes, you're not rich enough to leave first."

To the dismay of the Fishes and other refined old families, they had lost preeminence to two generations of prodigiously wealthy Johnny-come-latelies. These raw provincial millionaires could not be denied admission into capital-S society, the inner circle of glittering people who wintered in Palm Beach, summered in Newport or Bar Harbor, and visited London and Paris as casually as they dined at Delmonico's. Society was being democratized with alarming speed.

Indeed, money alone now made society go round—and at a hectic whirl. The very rich, armed with more cash than they had time to use, spent it competitively, to impress and to outdo one another. They shelled out millions for pompous mansions (*next page*) and huge steam yachts, and for indigent noblemen to wed their daughters. They kept dozens of servants, horses, and autos. In fact, it was said of one member of New York's fabulous Belmont clan that he kept "everything but the Ten Commandments."

Spicy accounts in the press of upper-crust shenanigans delighted gossip-column readers; the *pièces de résistance* for plutocrat-watchers were the parties of the very rich, especially their masked balls. To these spectacular functions the elite came by the giddy hundreds, wearing costumes that cost as much as $5,000 each. The hit of one ball was a small millionaire and his large wife, who came dressed up as a French king and a Norman peasant. Everybody roared when a malapropistic footman announced them to the guests as "Henry the Fourth and an enormous pheasant."

The shocking costs of such parties—$100,000 and up—troubled the conspicuously consuming rich less than the social complications involved in staging one. Even the most adroit hostess stretched her skills to mount a proper ball, coordinating the extra servants, wines, and perhaps a complete symphony orchestra to supply the music. It was small wonder that Mrs. Oliver Hazard Perry Belmont complained, "I know of no profession, art, or trade that women are working in today, as taxing on mental resource as being a leader of society."

A block-long town house, built by Cornelius Vanderbilt in flamboyant Gothic, was one of the four Vanderbilt mansions that graced Fifth Avenue in New York.

92nd Street

- Andrew Carnegie
- Archer M. Huntington
- Robert C. Lewis
- Henry Phipps

86th Street

- Mrs. Richard Dana
- Mrs. William Kingsland
- Lloyd S. Bryce

- Isaac Brokaw
- Payne Whitney
- J. Horace Harding
- Edward S. Harkness
- Alfred Pell
- Samuel Thorne

72nd Street

- Mrs. Edward H. Harriman
- Thomas Fortune Ryan
- George J. Gould
- Benjamin Thaw
- Mrs. Henry O. Havemeyer
- John Jacob Astor
- Mrs. James P. Kernochan
- Albert C. Bostwick
- Elbridge Gerry
- Mrs. Hermann Oelrichs

Plaza Hotel ■
(A.G. Vanderbilt)
Mrs. Cornelius Vanderbilt ■

57th Street

- Mrs. C.P. Huntington
- W.K. Brice and John F. Brice
- Levi P. Morton
- Cornelius Vanderbilt
- Mrs. H.M. Schieffelin
- Union Club

William K. Vanderbilt, Jr. ■
William K. Vanderbilt ■
Henry Clay Frick ■

Mrs. Ogden Goelet ■
Mrs. Russell Sage ■

- Miss Helen M. Gould

Sherry's ■   ■ Delmonico's

42nd Street

Fifth Avenue

Upper Fifth Avenue was New York's Gold Coast; the wealthy lined it with "French" châteaus and "Rhine" castles that excited the envy of anybody who wished to be somebody and the revulsion of those architects who advocated native originality. The map above locates some of the mansions and playgrounds of the very rich.

A duchess by marriage but dressed like a queen, Consuelo Vanderbilt wears the coronet of her husband's house of Marlborough to the coronation of Edward VII.

The Bartered Brides

When Consuelo Vanderbilt announced that she was to wed the Duke of Marlborough, her brother Harold blurted out, "He is only marrying you for your money."

That, alas, barely needed saying. Consuelo's mother, like dozens of other American millionaires, wanted a nobleman for her daughter. There were many eager candidates among Europe's impoverished nobility.

Though Consuelo was unwilling, her mother forced her to go through with the nuptials. Her spectacular New York wedding was a sober affair. Consuelo hung back for 20 minutes, alternately weeping and drying her tears, and when she finally appeared, "people were surprised to discover that she was fully half a head taller than the bridegroom."

Consuelo's marriage, like that of several other heiresses, was far from happy. But there was this consolation: What American money had joined together, it could almost as easily put asunder. Anna Gould (right, below) had no trouble acquiring *two* titled husbands: Count Boni de Castellane, a dapper French spendthrift, who cost the Goulds some $5.5 million before the match was dissolved in 1906; and, two years later, Boni's rich cousin Helie de Talleyrand-Périgord, Prince de Sagan. Handsome Alice Thaw (right, above), of the Pittsburgh railroad-and-coke Thaws, met her ticket to nobility, the impecunious Earl of Yarmouth, at a party in Washington, D.C. After a lavish wedding, the couple headed for a honeymoon in England, hotly pursued by a marshal eager to attach the Earl's baggage in lieu of bad debts. Adding to the commotion was the scandalous absence of Alice's brother Harry, who soon perpetrated an even greater scandal (overleaf).

The Countess of Yarmouth, nee Alice Thaw

The Princess de Sagan, nee Anna Gould

A Life cartoon (left) lampooned the figures in arranged matches: the heiress bound by her mother's will, the smallish nobleman, the preacher blind to the travesty.

Scandal of the Decade

On June 25, 1906, socialite Harry K. Thaw shot to death the famous architect Stanford White for trying to continue a dalliance with Thaw's bride, the winsome chorus girl Evelyn Nesbit *(left)*. The murder trial began in January 1907, and after weeks of lurid testimony, it ended with a hung jury. Thaw was retried the next year and adjudged "not guilty because insane." The high point of the affair came when Evelyn testified *(excerpt below)* in her husband's defense. As the scene begins, Evelyn has just described how she confessed to Thaw that White had "ruined" her when she was 16.

Lawyer: *What was the effect of this statement of yours upon Mr. Thaw?*
Evelyn: *He became very excited.*
Lawyer: *Will you kindly describe it?*
Evelyn: *He would get up and walk up and down the room a minute and then sit down and say, "Oh, God! Oh, God!" and bite his nails, and keep sobbing.*
Lawyer: *Sobbing?*
Evelyn: *Yes, it was not like crying. It was a deep sob. He kept saying, "Go on, go on, tell me the whole thing."*
Lawyer: *How long did that scene last, Mrs. Thaw?*
Evelyn: *Why, we stayed there all night. Every now and then he would come to me and ask me some particular thing about it.*
Lawyer: *In what direction were these questions?*
Evelyn: *He tried to find out whether Mama knew anything about it, and I said she did not. He thought, like a great many other people, that Mr. White was a very noble man. He told me that any decent person who heard that story would say it was not my fault. That I was simply a poor, unfortunate little girl, and that he did not think anything less of me. But on the contrary, he said that I must always remember he would be my friend, and no matter what happened, he would always be my friend.*
Lawyer: *When was it after that he renewed his proposal of marriage?*
Evelyn: *Later on. It was maybe two months after that he made up his mind and he was going to marry me anyway.*
Lawyer: *Will you please state to the jury that conversation?*
Evelyn: *I told him several times after that that even if I didn't marry him the friends of Stanford White would always laugh at him and make fun of him. I said marriage would not be a good thing—that I had been on the stage and I had been to a great many apartments with Stanford White.*
Lawyer: *What did he say to all these reasons of yours?*
Evelyn: *He kept saying he could not care for anybody else and could not possibly love anybody else; that his whole life was ruined; and he said he never would marry anyone else.*

Evelyn Nesbit, the chorus-girl wife of Harry Thaw, testified in his defense. But beneath her innocent beauty one spectator said he detected "an ice-cold brain."

Harry K. Thaw

Stanford White

"He kept saying he... could not possibly love anybody else."

Evelyn Nesbit

Cozy Cottages

In 1908, a tip-sheet for millionaire social climbers rated the resorts of the very rich. At the top of the list was glittering Newport—and the advice "be very careful." For here the plutocracy spent at a rate that could exhaust even a fair-sized fortune in a single season of eight to ten weeks.

The requisites for a summer in Newport began with a house, which the very rich called, without irony, a cottage. A cottage of 30 rooms could be built or bought for under a million dollars, but the architectural whims of the wealthy often ran up much greater expenses. Coal baron E. J. Berwind managed to spend nearly $1.5 million on his cottage, the Elms, but he was definitely put in the shade by the William K. Vanderbilts, who built their Marble House *(right)* for $2 million and furnished it for $9 million. Even

so, many connoisseurs held that the most luxurious of the cottages was Cornelius Vanderbilt's 70-room Renaissance palace, the Breakers *(below)*. A lifestyle befitting these mansions involved correspondingly fabulous sums. The biggest item was entertaining. Mrs. Pembroke Jones spent $300,000 a season on dinners and dances, and she was not the most imaginative of Newport hostesses. One candidate for that accolade was Mrs. Cornelius Vanderbilt; in 1902, it was her inspired fancy to import the whole cast of a New York hit, *The Wild Rose,* and to stage the show on her own lawn. But for sheer novelty, no one reached the heights—or the depths—of Harry Lehr, who invited 100 dogs and their masters to a banquet featuring fricassee of bones and shredded dog biscuit.

The Breakers cost Cornelius Vanderbilt $5 million before he bought a stick of furniture. Over its library fireplace was the motto, "Little do I care for riches."

Marble House, an $11 million gift from William K. Vanderbilt to his wife, was built of marble imported from Africa, and had a ballroom paneled in gold.

A setting for gourmands, the dining room of W. K. Vanderbilt's Newport cottage, Marble House, had solid bronze furniture and walls of Algerian marble.

Regal Seafarers

The 256-foot yacht North Star ferried the Vanderbilts between Newport and New York City, or took the family across the Atlantic to their European residences.

In Newport, yachting rather than horse racing was the sport of kings; indeed, nothing less than a king's ransom would buy a vessel of acceptable size and comfort. Cornelius Vanderbilt *(below, left)* paid about $250,000 for the *North Star (right)*, and every year the expenses of making the boat run put him another $20,000 or so out of pocket. The yacht owners expected speed as well as luxury; if a boat could not keep up with its rivals, it was scrapped for a new one. Albert C. Burrage built one of the most impressive. His *Aztec* could make 18.5 knots, and it carried 270 tons of coal, enough to travel 5,500 miles without a stop.

Commodore C. Vanderbilt

No less impressive than their performance and cost were the steam yachts' interiors. High ceilings, skylights, paneled walls, and parquet floors combined to give the impression that the owner had simply launched his mansion for a leisurely cruise. Many yacht owners had fully appointed offices on board, complete with a wireless to keep them in touch with Wall Street.

To yachtsmen, this effort and expense were worthwhile, for nothing could compare with the pleasure of a cruise in luxurious privacy. Financier J. P. Morgan, who ran through three big yachts aptly named *Corsair,* broke his customary silence to elaborate on the mystique of sailing. "You can do business with anybody," he said gruffly, "but you can only sail a boat with a gentleman." In keeping with this stern dictum, Morgan usually cast off with fewer than four men—not counting, of course, his 85-man crew.

The dining room of North Star was filled with Louis XIV furniture.

The fireplace in Vanderbilt's library was handsome but fake.

Mrs. Vanderbilt's stateroom was one of nine for guests and family.

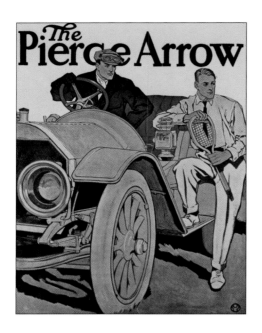

The 1910 Pierce Arrow (top) appealed to the white-shoed tennis set, while the Peerless competed for quality buyers by trading on its grandiloquent name.

Rich Man's Toy

By 1906, when the anxious statement below was issued by the president of Princeton, the recklessness of wealthy motorists had indeed aroused widespread resentment. Rich folk on their way to spas and shore resorts casually ran down livestock and drove on as fast as possible. In the cities, pedestrians were angered by the dangerous driving of millionaires like Alfred Gwynne Vanderbilt, who raced his red touring car through New York at reckless speeds of more than 10 miles an hour. Moreover, the plutocrats used their cars to flaunt their wealth.

> "Nothing has spread socialistic feeling in this country more than the use of the automobile. To the countryman, they are a picture of the arrogance of wealth, with all its independence and carelessness."
>
> Woodrow Wilson

As a magazine article reported, one rich member of an auto club "had the lamps on his Panhard gold plated, and on each of them the club emblem blazed. The emblems were solid gold, set with rubies."

Nevertheless, those who feared a socialistic backlash missed the mark by 180 degrees. The object of resentment became a symbol of success, coveted even by poor pedestrians; the automobile was admired all the more as new models incorporated greater elegance. Oldsmobile and other manufacturers prospered by making frank appeals to the pride of newly affluent people. The opulent car was usually powerful, and a few automakers began bragging about the speed of their products, as proved by glamorous races. But the car of the decade was the Great Arrow *(right);* it was so prestigious that its advertising snobbishly omitted all mention of cost ($4,500 and up). Whoever had to ask the cost obviously could not afford a Great Arrow.

THE GREAT ARROW

The Great Arrow
was so sure of its
stature that some
ads, like this one in
1907, grandly
omitted not only the
price but any de-
scription of the car.

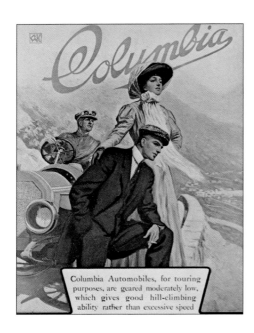

Columbia Automobiles, for touring purposes, are geared moderately low, which gives good hill-climbing ability rather than excessive speed

Columbia ads stressed traveling, as in the illustration at left of a European tour; of course such travelers needed some basic tools and supplies (right) before they were ready to go.

A Fad Becomes Fancy

While automobiling began as a haphazard adventure, the equipage for the new fad quickly became as elaborate as that for an English duke's safari into Africa. By 1904 a New York store, Saks & Co., found motoring garb a subject so complex that it required a 270-page catalog. The two Saks fashions shown here make it clear that women, as always, got the best of the couturier's art. The men, condemned to dusters resembling a chemist's laboratory coat, sought consolation in a catalog that was no less encyclopedic, put out by New York's posh hardware store, Hammacher Schlemmer. In 1906 that catalog urged every motorist to equip his car with a basic outfit of 35 tools, which could be bought for a mere $25.00. After a few more years of automotive inflation, a magazine recommended for the minimal motoring kit the formidable array of items listed on the opposite page.

Basic Tools and Supplies for the Early Automobilist

Tools

2 Pair tire chains

1 Efficient jack

1 Brace wrench for changing rims

1 Efficient tire pump

1 Tire gauge

1 Valve tool

1 Small vulcanizer

1 Sheet fine sandpaper

1 Sheet fine emery cloth

All special wrenches belonging to car

2 Monkey wrenches

1 Small set socket wrenches

1 Small Stillson wrench

2 Screw drivers (one with all wooden handle)

1 Pair pliers with wire cutters

1 Good jackknife

1 Small vise to clamp to running board

1 12-oz. machinist's hammer

1 Punch or carpenter's nail set

1 Cotter-pin extractor

1 Large flat mill file

1 Thin knife-edged file

1 Small short-handled axe

1 Towing cable

1 Oil squirt can

1 Grease gun

1 Small funnel

1 Chamois skin

1 Small ball of marline

1 Pocket electric flashlight (if car has no trouble lamp)

1 Pocket ammeter

Spare Parts & Extras

1 or 2 Extra tire casings and inner tubes

1 Strong two-gallon can extra gasoline

1 Strong two-quart sealable can gas-engine oil

1 Can grease

1 Small sealable can kerosene

1 Blowout patch

1 Leather tire sleeve

1 Package assorted cement patches

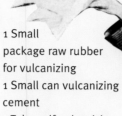

1 Small package raw rubber for vulcanizing

1 Small can vulcanizing cement

1 Tube self-vulcanizing cement

1 Can mastic

1 Box mica tire powder

6 or more extra tire valves

4 Extra valve caps

4 Extra dust caps

4 Extra headlight bulbs

2 Extra taillight bulbs

4 to 12 feet good insulated wire

1 Roll electrician's tape

1/2 as many extra spark plugs as motor has cylinders

1/2 as many extra porcelains as motor has cylinders

1 Ball asbestos wicking

1 Bundle waste

1 Assortment of gaskets to fit car

1 Piece radiator steam hose

2 Extra hose clips

2 Extra valve springs

1 Extra fan belt

1 Small sheet rubber packing

1 Assortment of cotter pins, nuts, lock washers, wood screws, and nails

Emergency Food Supply (Four People)

2 Two-gallon canvas water bags

4 Pound-packages hardtack

4 Half-pound cans meat or fish

2 Pounds sweet chocolate

2 Cans fruit

Personal luggage

An ad for the Locomobile, winner of the 1908 Vanderbilt Cup race, shifted the emphasis from elegance to speed as pioneer auto races caught the public fancy.

The Triumph of the Locomobile

The finish of the 1908 International Race for the Vanderbilt Cup. Won by the 90 H.P. Locomobile at an average speed of 64.38 miles an hour, breaking all records established in competition for this celebrated trophy. A victory for the Locomobile a triumph for the entire American automobile industry. The striking poster illustrated above is lithographed in eleven colors. Suitable for framing, with or without descriptive matter. Mailed on receipt of 10 cents.

1909 Locomobile Cars

The "30" LOCOMOBILE – A new five passenger model with a shaft drive system, thoroughly developed through three years of road testing. The name, Locomobile, on a shaft drive car guarantees its superiority. **$3500**

The "40" LOCOMOBILE – A seven passenger car, safe and comfortable – ideal for family use. The logical choice of those who want a high powered car. **$4500**

INFORMATION ON APPLICATION

The *Locomobile* Company of America. Bridgeport, Conn.

BRANCHES

NEW YORK – BOSTON – CHICAGO – PHILADELPHIA

Drivers rev up their motors for the start of the 1909 Indianapolis race. The 100-mile event was won by Louis Strang, with an average speed of 64 miles per hour.

Florodora Sextette and swains sing "Tell Me, Pretty Maiden," in "Florodora," the hit of 1900.

Showtime

⋆

ENTERTAINMENT FOR EVERYONE

In 1901 six-year-old Buster Keaton performed a vaudeville skit in which he teased his parents—who were, in fact, his real mother and father.

A Thousand Hits, Count 'Em

America was ravenous for entertainment as the new century got underway, and show business responded with a richer, more varied fare than the country had ever seen. Movies, sometimes called "flickering flicks" were in a groping infancy (a 1902 newsreel faked the eruption of a volcano by showing a beer barrel exploding in the sun). Spectacular circuses traveled from city to city in special trains of as many as 90 railway cars at a time. An inspired Tin Pan Alley sold two billion copies of sheet music in 1910 alone.

The legitimate stage achieved an all-time high of activity with more than 400 stock and touring companies carrying drama to the nation, and four or five plays opening on Broadway on an ordinary night. Many of these plays were of a new, earthy texture, and theater audiences, long used to lofty Shakespearean repertory and melodramas of the Jack Dalton genre, sometimes found themselves being brought down too far too fast. When, in a daring new production called *The City*, the word "goddam" was abruptly uttered—for the first time on a Broadway stage—the audience rose for an intermission in such horror and hysteria that the New York *Sun* critic fainted dead away in the ensuing crush.

For the average man of the decade, the favorite entertainment was vaudeville. Practically every town in the country had a vaudeville theater. Sometimes the performances lived up to their billing, and sometimes they did not even come close. Solid comedy acts like The Three Keatons *(right)*, with young Buster as The Human Mop, delighted audiences with their patter and knockabout acrobatics. On the other hand, reaction was decidedly mixed to the usual vaudeville collection of ventriloquists, jugglers, singers, and animal acts. The standard gags from rapid-fire comics—"I sent my wife to the Thousand Islands for a vacation: a week on each island" or "You can drive a horse to drink, but a pencil must be lead"—might receive any response from belly laughs to stony silence. And the Cherry Sisters, billed as "America's Worst Act," were indeed so bad that they always sang behind a net, which protected them from elderly fruit and vegetables thrown by the audience. On the following pages are samples of these performers, some of them the finest in the history of American theater. Others, like Adgie and Her Lions and the Southern Four, enjoyed merited obscurity.

Loie Fuller

Harry Lauder

Lew Fields

Joe Weber

Eva Tanguay

Adgie and her lion

Marie Dressler

The Southern Four

W. C. Fields

The Genius of Escape

It was a good thing he was on the right side of the law, because no straitjacket, no padlock, no chain, not even Scotland Yard, could contain the King of Handcuffs. Born Erik Weisz in Budapest, Harry Houdini baffled, delighted, and stunned audiences from London's vaudeville stages to the banks of Boston's Charles River. No restraint was too challenging, no predicament too perilous for his prodigious powers of escape. During one performance at Philadelphia's Keith Theater in 1905, Houdini accepted an impromptu challenge to escape from a straitjacket. The result, as described below in *Keith's Theater News,* was another victory for the great Houdini.

The audience gazed with breathless interest as the detectives, eager to triumph over the man who had triumphed so often over them, bound him up relentlessly.

In his good-natured way, Houdini remarked, "Please, gentlemen, give me a chance to breathe!"

"He'll never get out of that!" exclaimed a gentleman in the audience, and hundreds of heads around the speaker nodded their confirmation of the assertion.

What did Houdini do?

He smiled grimly, and then made an effort to move his crossed arms.

There was the slightest movement of the canvas jacket, and that was all!

Then he suddenly got down on the floor on his back, and the work of extricating himself began! It was an extraordinary effort of strength, skill, ingenuity, and intelligence. By several movements like those of a contortionist Houdini finally succeeded in working the jacket up to his head, thus partly releasing the tension on his crossed arms. After another severe struggle, he got one arm released, and then slipped out of the strap fastened between his legs. The rest of the work went on with a rapidity that was marvelous, and Houdini finally threw off the jacket in triumph!

Harry Houdini prepares to dive into Boston's Charles River bound in chains; an eager crowd gathers to see if the master magician can escape with his life yet again.

Bandits escape with the mail in one of the 14 scenes of *The Great Train Robbery*, whose famed director, Edwin S. Porter, pioneered in film editing.

A New Entry in Show Biz

I n 1903 a 12-minute epic called *The Great Train Robbery* became the first truly suspenseful movie. Photographed at a Lackawanna freight yard in Paterson, New Jersey, it set a permanent style for dramas that were depicted in several scenes. Within five years, 10,000 stores across the nation were converted into nickelodeons, small theaters that offered movies for a five-cent admission price.

Notices to the audience periodically appeared on the nickelodeon screens.

Medley for an Epoch

In the easy-going, almost unembarrassable mood of the first decade, songwriters tapped practically every emotion—and subject—in their efforts to score a hit. Pride in the technology of the age was evoked by songs like "In My Merry Oldsmobile" and "Come, Josephine, in My Flying Machine." Hearts were wrung by ballads such as "A Bird in a Gilded Cage" (the composer tested it out in a brothel to see if it would make the girls cry). Patriotic sentiment surged at the sound of George M. Cohan's "You're a Grand Old Flag," originally titled "You're a Grand Old Rag." Filial virtue found expression in "Next to Your Mother, Who Do You Love?"

The fountainhead of inspiration for the composers of the day was Tin Pan Alley, a block of 28th Street in New York City named for the sound of pianos pounding all day long. Music publishers on the Alley ground out thousands of tunes each year, but the business of picking a winner was woefully imprecise. Tin Pan Alley almost turned down "In the Good Old Summer Time" because publishers thought it would have audience appeal for only three months of the year. To their amazement, it sold a million copies in the first 12 months.

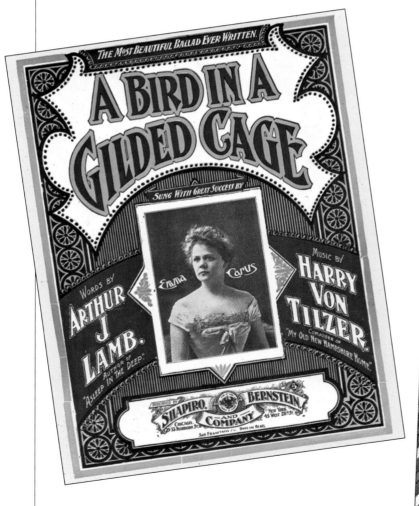

Young boys, surprised here by a photographer as they try to sneak under a canvas barrier, were surely the most avid and resourceful of circus fans.

The Big Top

Nothing in show business could match the excitement of a circus parade as it rolled through town luring customers with a display of ornately carved wagons, lumbering elephants and a calliope or "steam organ"—which brought up the rear because its boiler sometimes blew up. Dozens of circuses toured America, but the two giants were the Ringling Brothers Circus and Barnum & Bailey's, each striving to be recognized as the greatest show in the world. Barnum & Bailey's claimed to have an unexcelled "congress of wild beasts" in its menagerie. Ringling Brothers once asserted that it had the only giraffe left in the world.

The competition raised entertainment to dizzying heights. The circuses put on spectacular plays, such as the Ringling Brothers' *Jerusalem and the Crusades,* which used lavish scenery, hundreds of animals and more than a thousand performers. The three rings under the big top swarmed with clowns, lion trainers, and high-wire gymnasts. Earnest Clark, the fabulous trapeze artist, thrilled onlookers with his triple somersault. Isabella Butler rode in a toy automobile that sped down a ramp, turned upside down and shot "into space forty feet away across a veritable chasm of death." In the words of Barnum & Bailey's program, the audience reaction to such sights was bound to be pure awe: "Your heart still palpitates. 'This is the limit,' you say."

Ringling Brothers' posters boasted of equine acts (above) for, as Alf Ringling once said, "A circus without horses would be like a kite without a tail." Of course the same could be said of everyone's favorite circus animal, the elephant (below).

The Cambell Brothers Circus, a typical three-ring railroad circus, makes its debut performance of the 1909 season in the Kansas City Auditorium. In 1906, the height of circus popularity, there were 105 troupes touring the United States.

ACKNOWLEDGMENTS

The editors of this book wish to thank the following persons and institutions for their assistance:

Yeatman Anderson III, Public Library of Cincinnati and Hamilton County, Cincinnati, Ohio; Mrs. Lois Barland, Chippewa Valley Historical Society, Eau Claire, Wisconsin; Dr. John Blackburn, Hollywood, California; Mr. Boston Distiller, Inc., Roxbury, Massachusetts; Don Boyett, Managing Editor, *Amarillo Globe News,* Amarillo, Texas; James J. Bradley, Director, Automotive History Collection, Detroit Public Library; Beatrice Buda, Museum of the City of New York; Edwin H. Carpenter, Western Americana Bibliographer, Henry E. Huntington Library and Art Gallery, San Marino, California; Harry Collins, Brown Brothers, New York City; Mrs. Robert Crowe, Montebello, California; John Cumming, Director, Clarke Historical Library, Central Michigan University, Mt. Pleasant; Virginia Daiker, Prints and Photographs Division, Library of Congress; Mrs. Alice Dalligan, Curator of Manuscripts, Detroit Public Library; James Davis, Librarian, Western History Department, Denver Public Library; Mr. Richard A. Ehrlich, Boston; Mrs. Ruth K. Field, Curator of Pictures, Missouri Historical Society, St. Louis; Gibson House, Boston; The Gillette Company, Boston; Dorothy Gimmestad, Assistant Picture Curator, Minnesota Historical Society, St. Paul; Marshall Hail, *El Paso Herald-Post,* El Paso, Texas; Alison Kallman, New York City; Jack Krueger, Executive Editor, *Dallas Morning News;*

Thomas K. Leinbach, Administrator, The Historical Society of Berks County, Reading, Pennsylvania; Mrs. Alice Roosevelt Longworth; Helen MacLachlin, Curator, Theodore Roosevelt Birthplace, New York City; Mary Jane Maddox, *Marshall News Messenger,* Marshall, Texas; Mr. Elmo Mahoney, Dorrance, Kansas; Alexandra Mason, Director, Department of Special Collections and Mrs. Jane E. Riss, Curator, Regional History Division, University of Kansas Libraries, Lawrence; Robert D. Monroe, Chief of Special Collections Division, University of Washington Library, Seattle; Sol Novin, Culver Pictures, New York City; The Preservation Society of Newport County, Newport, Rhode Island; Mrs. Elizabeth Rademacher, Michigan Historical Commission Archives, Lansing; Stanley Rosenfeld, New York City; Janet Coe Sanborn, Curator, Cleveland Picture Collection, Ohio; Sy Seidman, New York City; Joseph W. Snell, Assistant State Archivist and F. R. Blackburn, Newspaper and Census Division, Kansas State Historical Society, Topeka; Claude Stanush, San Antonio, Texas; Gerald Talbot, Director, Museum Village of Smith's Clove, Monroe, New York; Mrs. Lawrence Tilley, Rhode Island Historical Society, Providence; John Barr Tompkins, Public Services Director, The Bancroft Library, University of California, Berkeley; Mrs. Judith Topaz, Assistant, Iconographic Collections, State Historical Society of Wisconsin, Madison; Gregory C. Wilson, Curator, Theodore Roosevelt Collection, Harvard College Library; Mrs. John A. Wipperfurth, Tomahawk, Wisconsin; Mrs. Geneva Kebler Wiskemann, Reference Archivist, Michigan Historical Commission Archives, Lansing.

PICTURE CREDITS

The sources for the illustrations in this book are listed below. Credits from left to right are separated by semicolons, from top to bottom by dashes.

Cover and dust jacket: Brown Brothers. **6, 7:** Chicago Historical Society. **8, 9:** Ford Archives: Henry Ford Museum, Dearborn, Michigan (Joe Clark). **10, 11:** Cleveland Public Library. **12, 13:** Culver Pictures. **14, 15:** Minnesota Historical Society. **16, 17:** Fred O. Seibel. **18, 19:** Atlanta Historical Society. **20, 21:** Culver Pictures. **22, 23** Library of Congress. **24:** Special Collections Library, University of Tennessee, Knoxville. **25:** Corbis. **26:** Underwood Photo Archives, SF—Brown Brothers. **27:** Jed Collectibles, Pemberton, NJ—Minnesota Historical Society—George Eastman House. **28, 29:** Pennell Collection, University of Kansas **30:** Courtesy the New York Historical Society (Robert Crandall). **31:** Corbis-Bettmann. **32:** Keystone View Company. **33:** Sy Seidman. **35:** Culver Pictures; Brown Brothers. **36:** Nebraska State Historical Society; Culver Pictures. **37:** Cincinnati Historical Society; U.S. Navy Photo. **38, 39:** Manchester Historical Society. **41, 42, 43:** Marie Cosindas. **44, 45:** Pennell Collection, University of Kansas. **46, 47:** Collection of Fred and Jo Mazzulla. **48, 49:** Western Collection, Denver Public Library. **50, 51:** The Byron Collection, Museum of the City of New York. **52:** Brown Brothers. **53:** Brown Brothers—Courtesy the Hearst Corporation. **54:** Bostwick-Frohardt Collection, owned by KMTV, Omaha—Culver Pictures. **55:** Edward Steichen, Museum of Modern Art—Bettmann Archive. **56:** Archive Photos. **58:** Bettmann Archive. **60, 61:** Culver Pictures. **62:** Photography by Karen Yamauchi for Chermayeff & Geismar Inc./Metaform Inc.. **63:** Brown Brothers. **64, 65:** New York Public Library. **66:** Brown Brothers—Photography by Karen Yamauchi for Chermayeff & Geismar Inc./Metaform Inc. **67:** Photography by Karen Yamauchi for Chermayeff & Geismar Inc./Metaform Inc. **68, 69:** Corbis. **70, 71:** Archive Photos. **72, 73:** Lewis W. Hine, George Eastman House. **74, 75:** Lewis W. Hine, George Eastman House. **76, 77:** Underwood & Underwood. **78:** Archive Photos. **79:** National Air and Space Museum, Smithsonian Institution. **80, 81:** Culver Pictures (2); Brown Brothers; Culver pictures (2); Brown Brothers. **82, 83:** Kansas State Historical Society. **84:** From *A Pictorial History of Aviation* by the editors of Year, (Photo World)—letter from *St. Nicholas* © 1908, The Century Co., reprinted by permission of Appleton-Century-Crofts, Division of Meredith Corp. **84, 85:** From *A History of Flight* by Courtlandt Canby, Charles Dollfus Collection. **86, 87:** United Press International. **88, 89:** Clarke Historical Library, Central Michigan University. **91:** Culver Pictures and Sy Seidman (Robert Crandall photo composition). **92, 93:** © King Features Syndicate 1907, 1909, Sy Seidman. **94, 95:** Sy Seidman and Culver Pictures (Robert Crandall photo composition). **97:** Sy Seidman. **98, 99:** Minnesota Historical Society. **100, 101:** City News Bureau Photo, St. Petersburg, Florida. **102:** Henry E. Huntington Library and Art Gallery. **103:** Brown Brothers. **104 through 117:** Kansas State Historical Society. **118, 119:** Culver Pictures. **120:** Missouri Historical Society. **121:** Brown Brothers. **122, 123:** From *Ladies' Home Journal,* September 15, 1910, © The Curtis Publishing Co., Culver Pictures. **124, 125:** From *L'Art de la Mode,* February 1906, Sy Seidman. **127:** From *Ladies' Home Journal,* July 1910, © The Curtis Publishing Co., Culver Pictures. **128:** Culver Pictures. **129:** Courtesy of Sears, Roebuck and Co. **130,131:** Items from the Bostwick-Braun Co. Hardware Catalogue, The Sears, Roebuck, & Co. Catalogue, 1906–1907, The Warshaw Collection, South Dakota State Historical Society, Charles J. Van Schaick Collection, State Historical Society of Wisconsin and The Eisinger, Kramer & Co. Catalogue 1899–1900. **132:** Culver Pictures. **133:** State Historical Society of Wisconsin. **134, 135:** The Byron Collection, Museum of the City of New York—Kansas State Historical Society, quote from *Ladies' Home Journal,* January 1910, © The Curtis Publishing Co. **136:** Culver Pictures—From *Life,* November 29, 1900. **137:** Sy Seidman. **139:** Brown Brothers. **140, 141, 143:** Culver Pictures. **144:** McGreevey Collection, Boston Public Library. **145:** National Baseball Hall of Fame Library, Cooperstown, NY. **146, 147:** Missouri Historical Society. **148:** Underwood & Underwood. **149:** Bettmann Archive. **150, 151:** Morris Rosenfeld & Sons. **153:** Brown Brothers. **154:** Culver Pictures. **156:** Brown Brothers. **157:** From *Life,* June 5, 1902; Culver Pictures—Brown Brothers. **158:** Culver Pictures. **159:** Brown Brothers—United Press International. **160, 161:** Evelyn Hofer. **162, 163:** Lee Boltin. **164, 165:** Morris Rosenfeld & Sons. **166:** From *Life,* February 17, 1910 (Hank Ehlbeck)—from *Life,* October 21,1909 (Hank Ehlbeck) **167:** From *Life,* August 15,1907 (Hank Ehlbeck). **168:** From *Life,* April 14, 1910 (Hank Ehlbeck); Automotive History Collection, Detroit Public Library. **169:** Automotive History Collection, Detroit Public Library. **170:** From *Life,* January 7, 1909, Sy Seidman. **171:** Automobile Manufacturers Association. **172, 173:** Brown Brothers. **175:** Sy Seidman. **176, 177:** Culver Pictures except bottom right (2) Brown Brothers. **178, 179:** Library of Congress. **180, 181:** Culver Pictures; cards by Sy Seidman. **182:** Sy Seidman. **183:** All Sy Seidman, except bottom right "School Days" by Will D. Cobb & Gus Edwards, © 1906 by Mills Music Inc. © Renewed 1934 by Mills Music Inc. (Culver Pictures); top right "My Wife's Gone to the Country, Hurrah, Hurrah!" by George Whiting, Irving Berlin and Ted Snyder. © 1909 Irving Berlin, © Renewed 1936 Irving Berlin, used by permission of Irving Berlin Music Corporation. **184:** Culver Pictures. **185, 186, 187:** Circus World Museum, Baraboo, Wisconsin.

BIBLIOGRAPHY

BOOKS

Allen, Frederick Lewis, *The Big Change*. Bantam Books, Inc., 1965.

Amory, Cleveland, *The Last Resorts*. Universal Library, Grosset & Dunlap, Inc., 1952.

Amory, Cleveland, *Who Killed Society?* Harper & Row Publishers, 1960.

Anderson, Rudolph E., *The Story of the American Automobile*. Public Affairs Press, 1950.

Atherton, Lewis, *Main Street on the Middle Border*. Quadrangle Books, Inc., 1966.

Balsan, Consuelo Vanderbilt, *The Glitter and the Gold*. Harper & Row Publishers, 1952.

Barrett, Richmond, *Good Old Summer Days*. D. Appleton-Century Co., 1941.

Blum, Daniel, *A Pictorial History of the Silent Screen*. Grosset & Dunlap, Inc., 1953.

Canby, Henry Seidel, *American Memoir*. Houghton Mifflin Co., 1947.

Cantor, Norman F., and Michael S. Werthman, eds., *The History of Popular Culture*. Macmillan Company, 1968.

Churchill, Allen, *The Great White Way*. E. P. Dutton & Co., Inc., 1962.

Cohn, David L., *Combustion on Wheels*. Houghton Mifflin Co., 1944.

Cohn, David L., *The Good Old Days*. Simon and Schuster, Inc., 1940.

Corsi, Edward, *In the Shadow of Liberty*. Macmillan Company, 1935.

Eliot, Elizabeth, *Heiresses and Coronets*. McDowell, Obolensky, 1959.

Ewen, David, *The Life and Death of Tin Pan Alley*. Funk & Wagnalls Co., 1964.

Faulkner, Harold U., *The Quest for Social Justice 1898–1914*. Macmillan Company, 1931.

Fox, Charles Philip, *A Ticket to the Circus*. Superior Publishing Co., 1959.

Freudenthal, Elsbeth, *Flight into History, The Wright Brothers and the Air Age*. University of Oklahoma Press, 1949.

Fulton, A. R., *Motion Pictures*. University of Oklahoma Press, 1960.

Hagedorn, Hermann, ed., *The Roosevelt Family of Sagamore Hill*. Macmillan Company, 1954.

Howe, Edgar Watson, *The Story of a Country Town*. Twayne Publishers, 1962.

Hughes, Glenn, *A History of the American Theatre, 1700–1950*. Samuel French, Inc., 1951

Johnston, William Davison, *T.R.: Champion of the Strenuous Life*. Farrar, Straus & Cudahy, 1958.

Langford, Gerald, *The Murder of Stanford White*. Bobbs-Merrill Co., Inc., 1962.

Laurie, Joe Jr., *Vaudeville*. Henry Holt & Co., 1953.

Lord, Walter, *The Good Years*. Bantam Books, Inc., 1965.

Mattfeld, Julius, *Variety Music Cavalcade, 1620–1961*. Prentice-Hall, Inc., 1962.

May, Earl Chapin, *The Circus from Rome to Ringling*. Dover Publications, Inc., 1963.

Mayer, Grace, *Once Upon a City*. Macmillan Company, 1958.

Morris, Lloyd, *Not So Long Ago*. Random House, Inc., 1949.

Morris, Lloyd, *Postscript to Yesterday*. Random House, Inc., 1947.

Roosevelt, Theodore, *An Autobiography*. Charles Scribner's Sons, 1946.

Smith, Cecil, *Musical Comedy in America*. Theatre Arts Book, 1950.

Spaeth, Sigmund, *A History of Popular Music in America*. Random House, Inc., 1948.

Steffens, Lincoln, *The Shame of the Cities*. Peter Smith, 1948.

Stern, Phillip Van Doren, *A Pictorial History of the Automobile*. Viking Press, Inc., 1953.

Wagenknecht, Edward, *The Seven Worlds of Theodore Roosevelt*. Longmans, Green & Co., 1958.

Wheeler, Thomas C., ed., *A Vanishing America: The Life and Times of the Small Town*. Holt, Rinehart & Winston, Inc., 1964.

White, William Allen, *Forty Years on Main Street*. Farrar & Rinehart, 1937.

Whitehouse, Arch, *The Early Birds*. Doubleday & Co., Inc., 1965.

Year editors, Flight, *A Pictorial History of Aviation*. Year, Inc., 1953.

INDEX

Numerals in italics indicate an illustration of the subject mentioned.

A

Advertisements: automobile, *166-170*; circus, *185*; corsets, *120*; drugs, regulation of, 129; Sears, Roebuck, 129

Agriculture, *114-117*; employment, *table 36*; mechanization, 29, *115*

Airplanes, early, *76-77, 78, 79-83*

Alcohol consumption, 45

American Indian population figures (1900 vs. 1996), *table 35*

American League (baseball), 142, 144

Army football team, 142

Arrow automobiles, *166-167*

Astor, John Jacob, 155

Atlantic City, New Jersey, 102

Automobile
See Car

Aviation, beginnings of, *76-77, 78, 79-87*

B

Baldwin, Thomas Scott, dirigible of, *86-87*

Barbershop, *46-47*

Barnum & Bailey's, 184; poster, *185*

Baseball, 102, 142, *144*

Baseball cards, 90, *91*

Basketball, women's, *118-119*

Beaches, *6-7*, 102

Beard, Daniel Carter, 90

Belmont, Mrs. Oliver Hazard Perry, 152

Bender, Chief, 142

Berwind, E.J., 150

Boating, 152, *164-165*; club, *38-39*

Bok, Edward, 129; quoted, 134

Bossism, 72

Boston, Massachusetts: first World Series games in, *144-145*; saloons, 45

Boston *Herald*, quoted, 24

Boxing, 142, 148, *149*

Boy Scouts, 90

Broadway shows, 174

Bryan, William Jennings, *54*

Budget, national, *table 37*

Burrage, Albert C., 164

Busbey, Katherine G., quoted, 120, 123

Business, 24; attitudes toward labor, 28, 33; big, T.R.'s curbing of, 57; mail-order, 129-131; marketing, 27, 129; ruthlessness, 23; small town,

108-111; statistics (1900 vs. 1996), *table 37*

Buster Brown (comic strip), *92-93*

Butler, Isabella, 184

C

Canals, *16-17*, 57; trade, decline, 27

Captain and the Kids, The (comic strip), 92

Car(s), *166-171*; accident deaths (1900 vs. 1996), *table 36*; advertisements, *166-170*; models, *166-167*; motorists' fashions, *168-169*; ownership statistics (1900), 24; prices of, 166; racing, 166, *170-171*; recklessness of motorists, 166; of the rich, 166; tools and supplies, *table* 169; transcontinental tour, *20-21*

Cartoons: futuristic views, *35*; money-title marriages, *157*

Castellane, Count Boni de, 157

Chicago, Illinois: immigrants in, 28, 62, 72; population, 28; saloons, 45

Chicago Athletic Club, 146, 147

Child labor, 23, 33,134

Children: discipline, 90; infant

mortality, *table 36*; pastimes of, 90, *91-103, 103* in school, table 8, 88-89,90,98-101

Circus, 174, *184-187*

Cities: growth, 26, 28-31; immigrants in, 28, 62, *68-75*; population figures (1900 vs. 1996), *table 34*

Clarke, Ernest, 184

Cleveland, Grover, quoted, 40

Cleveland, Ohio, *10-11*; growth, 28; immigrants in, 70; municipal reforms, 70

Clothing: men's, 40, *41*; motoring outfits, *168-169*; prices, 124; ready-to-wear, 123,124,129; women's, 120,123,*124-125*

Clubs: men's, 40-45, 46-47, *46-47, 140-141*; women's, 134, *135*

Cobb, Tyrus Raymond, 142

Cohan, George M., 182

College football, 142, *143*

Columbia automobile, *168*

Comic strips, 90, *92-93*

Corsets, *120*, 123

Corsi, Edward, quoted, 64

Cosmopolitan, The, quoted, 102

Cosmopolitan Saloon, Telluride, Colorado, *46-47*

Cotton marketing, *18-19*
"Cross-of-gold" speech, Bryan, 54
Cuba, 53, 57
Curtiss, Glenn, *80*

D

Dalton, Jack, 174
Davis, Richard Harding, *54*
Daytona Beach, Florida, *6-7*
Death, leading causes of, *table 36*
Depew, Chauncey, quoted, 23
Detroit Tigers, 142
DeWitt, John, 147
Dime novels, *94-95*, 96, *97*
Dinneen, Bill, 144
Dirigibles, *84-85*, *86-87*
Diseases, 34; leading causes of
   death, *table 36*
Divorce statistics (1900 vs. 1996),
   table 36
Dixon, Cromwell, *84*; dirigible of,
   84-85
Dorrance, Kansas, *104-105*, *106-
   117*
Douglass, Mrs. Gordon, *153*
Dressler, Marie, *177*
Drug regulation, 57,129
Dunne, Finley Peter, quoted, 120
Durhamville, New York, *16-17*

E

Edison, Thomas Alva, quoted, 83
Education, statistics (1900 vs.
   1996), *table 35. See also* Schools
Edward VII, King, 156
Ellis Island, immigrants at, *60-61*,
   62, *63-65*
Employment: in government
   (1901 vs. 1995), *table 37*;
   major industry statistics (1900
   vs. 1996), *table 36*; of men, *table
   36*; sample occupations statistics
   (1900 vs. 1996), table 36; of
   women, *table 36*, 124, *132-133*
Entertainment, *172-173*, 174, *175-
   187*; circus, 174, *184-187*; high
   society, 152, 160, *164-165*;
   movies, 174, *180-181*; music,
   102, *182-183*, ; theater, 174;
   trolley parks, 102; vaudeville,
   102, 174, *175-177*
Erie Canal, *16-17*, 27
Evans, George ("Honey Boy"), 102

F

Family statistics (1900 vs. 1996),
   table 36
Farm life, *14-15*, 29, *114-117*
Farming. See Agriculture
Fashions: men's, 40, *41* motoring,
   168-169; women's, *120-125*
Federal budget, *table 37*
Feminist movement, 124
Fields, Lew, *176*
Fields, W. C., *177*
Financial panic of 1907, 55
Fire departments, 45, *48-49*

Fish, Mrs. Stuyvesant, 152
Fiske, Harrison Grey, *51*
Florodora (show), *172-173*
Flyer (Wright brothers' plane), *81*
Food: prices, 24, *table 29*; regula-
   tion, 57,173
Football, 142, *143*
Fourth of July parades, *12-13*
Frank Merriwell dime novels, *94,
   95, 96, 97*
Fuller, Loie, *176*
Furniture, *130-131, 162-163, 164-
   165*; prices, 130-131

G

Gale, Zona, quoted, 28
Gary, Elbert H., 31
Gibson, Charles Dana, *136*, 138,
   139; Gibson girl,*136-137*, 138,
   139
Goelet, Mrs. Odgen, 155
Gould, Anna (Princess de Sagan),
   157
Grand Rapids, Michigan, 26
Great Arrow automobile, 166, *167*
Great Train Robbery, The, 180-181
Grocery, *28-29*; prices, 29, *table 29*

H

Hadley, Clifton O., 81
Halbe, Leslie, 107
Handy Books, Beard, 90
Hanna, Mark, quoted, 23, 57
Harvard football team, 142, *143*
Hearst, William Randolph, *53*, 90
Helicopter, of A. E. Hunt, *82-83*
Heston, Willie, 142
Hillis, Newell Dwight, quoted, 23
Houdini, Harry, *178, 179*

I

Ibsen, Henrik, 120
Immigrants, 62, *63-75*; assimila-
   tion of second generation, 72;
   attitudes toward, 62; in city
   slums, 28, 62, *68-75*; countries
   of origin, *table 35-36*; at Ellis Island, *60-61*, 62, *63-65*; political
   machines and, 72
Immigration statistics: breakdown
   by national origin (1900 vs.
   1996), *table 35*; 19th Century,
   26, 27; 1900-1910, 28, 62; number returning home, 62
Income statistics: average annual,
   of industrial labor (1900), 33;
   average hourly wage, *table 36*;
   average weekly pay, *table 36*, 40,
   62; high government offices
   (1900 vs. 1996), *table 37*
Indianapolis auto race (1909), 171
Industry: employment, table 36;
   growth, 24-26; top companies
   (1909), *table 9*
Interior decorating, *130-131*; society mansions, *162-163*; society
   yachts, *164-165*

J

James, Henry, quoted, 23, 102
Jeffries, Jim, 142, 148, *149*
Jetmore, Kansas, *82-83*
Johnson, Byron Bancroft, 144
Johnson, Jack, 142, 148, *149*
Johnson, Tom L., 70
Journalism: muckrakers and ex-
   poses, 33, 70, 72, 129; yellow, 53

K

Keaton, Buster, 174, *175*
Keeler, Willie, 142
Kitty Hawk, North Carolina,
   Wright brothers' first flight at,
   76-77, 78

L

Labor: average annual wages
   (1900), 33; average hourly
   wages, *table 36* ; average weekly
   wages, *table 36*, 62; child, 23,
   33,134; exploitation of, 33; farm
   vs. factory, 1900 statistics, *table
   36*; major industry statistics
   (1900 vs. 1996), *table 36*; occupation statistics (1900 vs. 1996),
   table 36; unemployment, *table
   36*; working hours, *table 36*, 62
Ladies' Home Journal, The, 127,
   129; quoted, 134
Langley, Samuel, flight experiment
   of, 78, *79*
*L'Art de la Mode and le Charme
   United*, 123
Lauder, Harry, *176*
Lee, Viscount, quoted, 59
Lehr, Harry, 152, 160
Life (old humor magazine), *136*;
   cartoon, *157*; Gibson serials, 136
Lodge, Henry Cabot, 62
London, Jack, *148*; quoted, 148
Longworth, Alice Roosevelt. *See*
   Roosevelt, Alice
Lorz, Fred, 146, 147
Los Angeles, California, growth, 29

M

McClure's magazine, 72
McCurdy, John A.D., *81*
McGraw, James J., 31
McGuffey, William Holmes, 99
McGuffey's *Readers*, 28, 90, 99
McKinley, William, 54, 57
Magazines, women's, 120, 126, *127*
Mail-order business, 129-131
Manchester, New Hampshire, *38-
   39*
Marble House (Vanderbilt man-
   sion), 160, *161-163*
Marietta, Georgia, *18-19*
Marlborough, Duchess of (Con-
   suelo Vanderbilt), *156*, 157
Marlborough, Duke of, 157
Marriage, of heiresses, with nobil-
   ity, 152, 157
Martin, W.H., *80*

Martinette (Martin plane), *80*
Men: employment statistics (1900
   vs. 1996), *table 36*; fashions, 40,
   41; grooming aids, *42*;
   life expectancy of (1900 vs.
   1996), *table 36*; pastimes of, *44-
   45, 46-51*; superior status of, 40;
   women outnumbered by, in
   1900, 40
Mississippi River, decline of river
   trade, 27
Montgomery Ward, 129
Morgan, J. Pierpont, *55*; quoted,
   164; yachts of, 164
Movies, 174, *180-181*
Muckrakers, 33, 70, 72
Music, hit songs, *182-183*

N

National League (baseball), 142,
   144
Nesbit, Evelyn (Mrs. Harry K.
   Thaw), *158, 159*
New York Athletic Club, *140-141,
   146-147*
New York City, *8-9*; Broadway
   shows, 174; futuristic view of,
   30; immigrants in, 28, 62, *68-69*,
   72, *74-75*; high society man-
   sions on Fifth Avenue, *154-155*;
   men's clubs, 45; population, 28;
   population projections, 31; Tin
   Pan Alley, 174, 182; T.R. as po-
   lice commissioner of, 57
New York *Morning Journal*, 53
New York *World*, quoted, 136
Newcomb, Simon, quoted, 78
Newport, Rhode Island, 152, *153*
   160, 164; mansions, *160-163*
Newspapers, 24; yellow journal-
   ism, 53
Nick Carter dime novels, *94*, 95
Nickelodeon, 181
Nome, Alaska, Fourth of July,
   12-13
Norris, Frank, quoted, 70
North Pole, Peary at, 52
North Star, the (yacht), *164-165*

O

Occupations, sample statistics
   (1900 vs. 1996), *table 36*
Oldsmobile, 166
Olympics, 142, *146-147*

P

Paducah, Kentucky, 27
Palm Beach, Florida, 152
Panama Canal, 58
Panic of 1907, 55
Parties, high society, 152, 160
Patent medicines, 129, *130*
Patten, George, 95
Peary, Robert E., *52*
Penrod, Tarkington, 90
Philadelphia, Pennsylvania, 72;
   population, 28